THE ART OF 14-18s

AGE RANGE TOOLS FOR LEADING GROUPS

Toolbag Contents

GW01403037

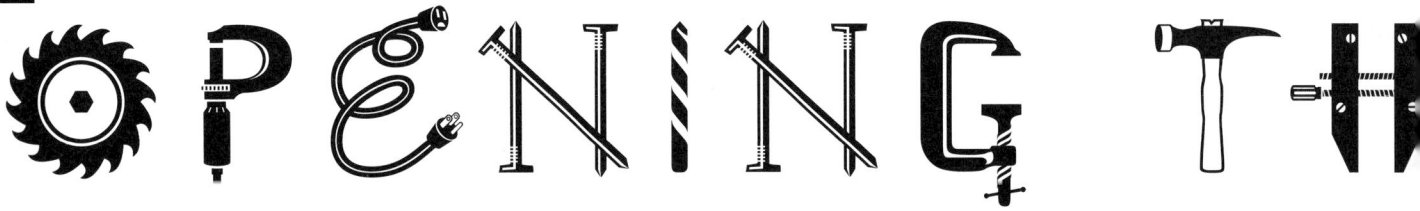

A youth leader needs many pockets – from the one holding the huge bunch of church hall keys to the one containing an inexhaustible supply of relevant jokes and stories.

Here are ten pockets full of wisdom. Not the wisdom of the 'know-it-all', but the wisdom of some experienced youth leaders who, by God's grace, have stuck around for a while. Rummage in their pockets (oo er!) and see what valuables you can find.

Don't get the wrong idea – reading this book won't make life a bed of roses. Teenagers can be a joy to work with. The same teenagers can also be selfish and inconsistent. You may often feel taken for granted, or even pretty desperate.

On top of this, not even the Bible talks explicitly about working with the age group. A bit of a shame, really.

SO WHY BOTHER?

The Bible does, however, have a lot to say about working with *people*, and we can assume that fourteen to eighteen year olds fall into this category! Everything written in the Bible about spreading the gospel and making disciples is about your group.

Their ability to respond to the gospel and to be disciples is amazing. Their commitment can be hard to win, but once it's there they can put the rest of us to shame. They will be developing their own style, but will be prepared to try out all sorts of new ideas. Many are still vulnerable and will want to share their life with you – and they'll expect you to share yours with them. And most will question and explore what people tell them, rather than simply accepting what they hear. This is all brilliant news for you as a leader.

And just think – the younger they become Christians the longer they will have to be God's ambassadors and to build up the Church! So, in spite of the struggles, you are involved in exciting, strategic work for God's kingdom. That is why you should bother with fourteen to eighteens.

HOW THE 'TOOLBAG' WORKS

The *Toolbag* series is designed to help you (and other leaders in your church) to explore issues that are vital to your children's and youth ministry. You will have the opportunity to

see what the Bible says on the issues and explore the issues on your own or with others

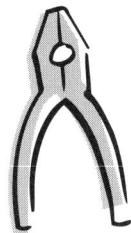

pray about them

get some off-the-peg, practical ideas

make your own notes which will lead you to action

hear real-life stories of people and churches that are tackling the issues

WOW!

be reminded of what you have learnt.

THE RIGHT TOOLS

A toolbag has pockets which contain tools – that is obvious. You will need to rummage through each pocket to find exactly the right tool for the job you have to do. No toolbag does the work for you... at least we haven't found one yet that does! So here are the tools – the rest is up to you, to others in your church, and to God.

NEED A HAND?

If you are the only leader working with your group, you are still a team – with God! Try to set aside enough time, on a regular basis, to work through the toolbag. Realistically, in order to make room in your busy schedule, you may have to drop some of your other reading. Since there will be Bible exploration to do, the toolbag could, for instance, take the place of your normal Bible reading, in the short term.

If you do have other leaders in your team, make sure you meet regularly with them. You could use the material in one pocket of this toolbag as the first half of a meeting, with your normal planning and discussion handled much more quickly than usual in the second half.

WHO IS IT FOR?

This toolbag is for all leaders of church-based youth groups, whether you're just starting or you feel you've been doing the job for ever. The early pockets are intended to be of particular use before you start leading a group; others will help you develop your skills in the months that follow.

Alternatively, if you are already experienced as a leader, you could use this toolbag for your planning and training for a whole year, as a refresher course to help you brush up on the basics.

GETTING STARTED

So make a date with yourself to start in Pocket 1.

Or plan a time to get together with your other leaders. Search through the pockets yourself first to select the tools that will be most helpful to you all.

We hope you will not only survive with your group, but thrive. God has plans for the experience to be good news for you, your group, the Church and, ultimately, the whole world. Go on, think big!

WHAT'S IT ALL ABOUT?

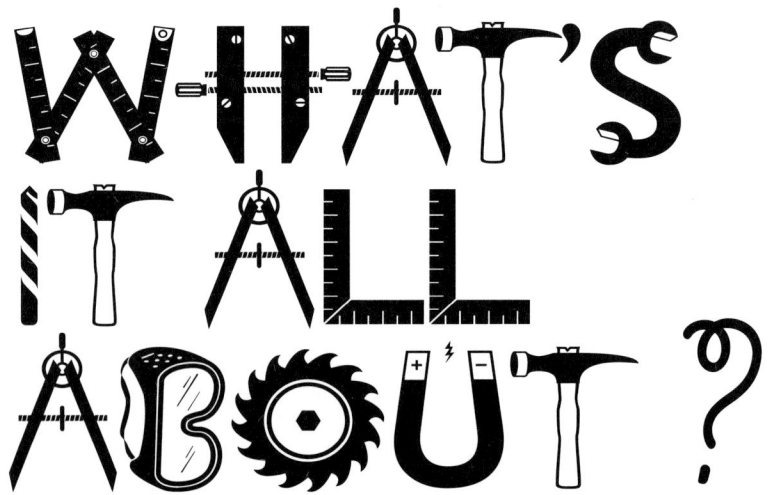

WHY IS YOUTH WORK SO IMPORTANT?

Bodies must be firm, fit and fantastic; so the advertisers tell us. Rubbish, of course, in a lot of ways. But the Church is a body – Christ's body – and without youth work it is not just sadly flabby but it is missing an important and valuable limb. If teenagers are not cared for in church, the work in younger age groups may come to nothing. Those who have not had church involvement in their teens are less likely to come into the body at a later age. And in twenty or thirty years' time – where's the body?

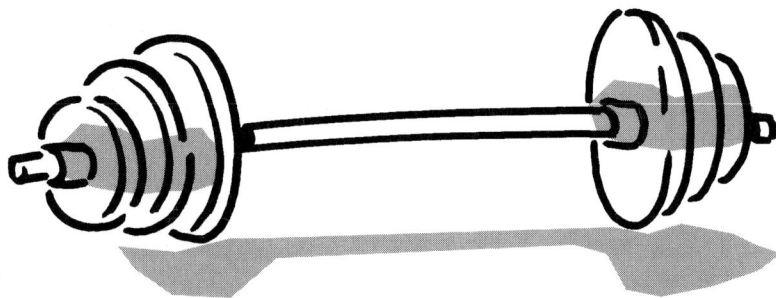

Be in no doubt that leading this age group can be tough! Older teenagers can be emotionally demanding, physically challenging, with an often alien culture of their own, with sexual and psychological problems all too close to adult ones and with an insatiable appetite for the time and support of their leaders. Committed, spiritual leadership is therefore fundamental to this work, is hard to find and is vital to maintain.

So it's hard but crucial work. We'll need to build on a firm foundation. What principles will we base it on?

1 Belief in the power of prayer, as the mainstay of youth work

2 Belief in the power of the Bible, as the backbone of the teaching programme

3 Belief in the power of the simple gospel, as the central attraction of youth work

4 Belief in the importance of the individual, as the practical guideline for the pastoring of the group

5 Belief in the fellowship of the Body, as the necessary context for growth for a young Christian.

These vital principles underlie just about everything in this book.

We must never allow youth work to be treated in isolation from the rest of the Church. The Bible knows nothing of 'youth' as a separate category for ministry, although it is clear that young people (such as David, Josiah, Mary and many others) are both valuable and useful to God. We need to see young people as members of their families, of

GENUINELY INTERESTED

LUKE 10:1

LUKE 6 12-16

LUKE 9:28

JOHN 21:15-19

society and of today's (not tomorrow's) Church. This will influence all our thinking about youth ministry and will require us to be bridges rather than barriers between the young people and the Church. Our aim will always be to build up the body of Christ. This will help keep our eyes on mature Christian disciples emerging from the top end of our youth group, rather than on the number of young people our programme is attracting.

What should be our approach? Quality, not quantity, is the key. Thousands came to hear Jesus preach but he told them parables to sieve the genuinely interested from the idly curious. Of the genuinely interested, he chose 70 (Luke 10:1). Of the 70, he chose 12 (Luke 6:12-16). Of the 12, he selected 3 for special attention (Luke 9:28). Of these, he gave a special commission to just one (John 21:15-19). If Jesus focused his ministry in this way it will be a fruitful pattern for us to follow.

So we need to concentrate on working from the centre outwards. We can probably help, at a deep level, far fewer people than we expect. But if we pastor the key ones as God means us to, he will use them to bless others.

What will this mean in practice? First, a central concern is to nurture our core group, so that they grow and develop as disciples. Whatever pattern and programme we have for nurture, it is crucial that we are not side-tracked from it, nor discouraged if numbers affected appear small.

If the core are our 'committed' people, we need to create opportunities for a further group of 'interested' people to grow around them. Such a contact group may exist naturally, but it will be important for us to foster these opportunities. Evangelism is a continuous and corporate activity. So there needs to be some aspect to our programme which encourages and allows the 'interested' to move into the 'committed' group. The process will

usually be gradual, but there must be opportunities on the way for individuals to be confronted by Jesus and respond personally to him.

There is no universal pattern for youth work, whether church-based or not. Every group is different, just as every church is different, every pub is different, every arcade is different and everywhere else where young people meet is different. It is important to work out an appropriate pattern for each situation, to review it regularly and to alter it ruthlessly if it does not work.

Whatever the pattern, it should be constructed around certain key elements:

● imparting knowledge. Aim for a planned, balanced teaching programme, presented in lively, varied ways.

● imparting skills. These will be skills of Christian growth, such as prayer and handling the Bible, and social skills. The latter, which might include skills of discussion, presentation, group work and so on, are valuable in their own right but our motivation for imparting them will be linked to their usefulness in conveying Christian truth.

● changing hearts and attitudes. This is most important of all, and a case of 'caught rather than taught'. Attitudes are learnt from life. Young people learn them from their peer group, so we must work to create a warm, open, attractive, Christ-centred group. But teenagers also learn attitudes from significant adults around them, so we must be prepared for 'life-to-life' discipling. This will mean opening our lives and homes to group members; it can be painful and tiresome but equally it can be thrilling and it opens up great opportunities for the gospel. We will go on outings with the young people, we will take them away to residential situations and we will model Christianity to them in all we do. They will learn far more about obedience to authority from seeing the way we drive our cars than from all our teaching sessions on the subject; they will learn more about a Christian attitude to possessions from our homes than from all our sessions on 'worldliness'.

WOW!

Start as you mean to go on, with the spiritual aim clear and explicit. Don't delay starting because numbers are small or leadership weak. A little Bible study of three or four people has been the seed of many powerful youth works.

AIMS

Deciding on the aim of our work can be difficult but it's essential to be clear about it before we start the work.

Imagine three people (let's call them A, B and Tarquin), each with a ball which they want to throw into a bucket. A throws the ball at random and then moves the bucket to where the ball stops. Result: failure to achieve the aim. B places a hundred buckets in a tight group and then throws the ball at the group. Result: failure to know whether the ball is in the right bucket. Tarquin places the bucket carefully, practises throwing the ball, takes aim and gets the ball into the bucket. Result: aim achieved.

That may seem a daft example, but think of the ball as our work and the bucket as what we want to achieve. If we don't know what this is and how to get there, what chance do we have? We'll end up either having to pretend that where we happen to end up is where we always intended (A), or with no idea at all whether we've done anything worthwhile (B).

So what should we be aiming at? **Life** and **growth**, just about sum it up. We want to see young people reconciled to God through Jesus and presented to him perfect on the last day (see Colossians 1:22, 28). And because we don't know when this presentation will take place, the work is urgent! So we will use all our gifts and energy to interest, intrigue and involve our young people – but these things are means to our end, not aims in themselves. Christian youth work is not about entertainment, although it will often be entertaining. It is not a social education programme, although it will often enhance the social skills of those with whom we work. It is certainly not about crowd control, although we will model and encourage self-discipline and godliness. Through such things we aim to bring young people into relationship with the living God and to help them in their early steps along the life-long path of obedience, holiness and witness. Phew!

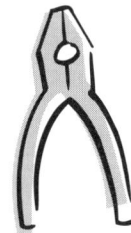

Read Colossians 1:21-23. Think how it applies to your own life and give thanks to God for what he has done for you. Now pray these verses through for the young people with whom you work or will work, thinking of them by name wherever possible.

WHAT DO I GET OUT OF IT?

Disappointment

It was a badly attended, Wednesday night Bible study group. We were looking at 'gifts' and trying to work out what 'discernment' was. Charlotte said, '...helping people with their Holy Spirit problems.' It was a wonderful definition. But for Charlotte the next few years involved her parents splitting up and her mother's long, terminal illness. Despite her remarkable spiritual insight as a teenager, by her early twenties she had positioned herself outside the company of believers.

'A youth leader needs an endless capacity for disappointment' (Pam Harvey, CPAS Regional Consultant for the Centre of England). If you can't handle disappointment, don't do youth work. Anything in which we invest emotions, energy, effort and time runs the risk of sometimes exposing us to desperate sadness and the feeling that we're wasting our time. This seems to be particularly true of youth work. It may be something to do with working with volatile, questioning people; it may be that we've been through that time of life and think we know the way they should take; it may be something else. We need to make sure that we have appropriate support from the church and our fellow leaders, and that we provide them with our support.

Fulfilment

The other side of the coin! When it goes well, it's wonderful! People's lives are changed, their eternal destiny is changed, their witness about the Lord is changed, and God in his grace allows us to be agents in bringing these things about.

A crown of life

Read 1 Peter 5:1-4. We can legitimately apply this word written to 'elders' to our own situation. What does Peter say we should be like in our role as 'shepherds' of our young flock? What characteristics should we *not* display? Pray through this list. Then thank God for the crown of glory that awaits us. We may not always be sure that we're doing things quite right – but that crown will be unmistakable. We may face disappointments – but they will fade, and our crown never will.

WHO SHOULD BE INVOLVED?

TEAM TALK

In running any youth work, the ideal is to recruit a team of leaders rather than going it alone.

Q. Why is a youth work without a team of leaders like a one-legged elephant?

Obvious A. Because it doesn't make much progress and could come crashing down at any moment.

Finished chortling? Hadn't started? Never mind, it's a serious point. Teams are, in most cases, preferable to going it alone, and not only when it comes to legs.

What are the great advantages of doing youth work in a team? This is not an exhaustive list, but it's a pretty good place to start:

● Relationships can be built with more people than we can achieve alone, and different personality types can be reached by suitable team members

● More gifts can be contributed to the work and there is less pressure to become an expert in everything

● There is less danger of group members turning into clones of a particular leader if they have a range of Christian models to relate to

● Pressures are spread

● Ideas are pooled

● Vision is sharpened

● Handing over the work can be a smoother and more positive process than suddenly having to introduce a complete stranger

● Teams allow fuller and more accurate evaluation of the work than one person's view

● Being in a team gives us a chance to live out Christian relationships: a vital witness to our group.

Meeting to pray and plan in a team keeps the work varied, refreshed and focused. Prayer and planning are part of the work, not just add-ons which can help it, so this is important.

Teams are not magic. They bring their own extra strains and commitments and sometimes we'll probably wish everyone else would just go away and leave us to get on with things on our own. However, they're a great tool for getting God's vital work done.

If you can't find any other leaders, do the work anyway while you pray for them to be provided. It's God who gives us the strength for the work (2 Corinthians 12:9) and he can bless one leader working alone just as he can a team. But be discoverable. Thomas Hamilton did a lot of youth work on his own and eventually carried out the Dunblane massacre. Try to have another adult around, even if they're not a leader.

WHAT IS A LEADER LIKE?

Do you need to wear a baseball cap and big trainers? Or a top hat and tails? Or whatever the current youth fashion has

turned to in the time between this being written and your reading it? Well, no. It's much more important that you should *like* teenagers than that you should *be like* them.

Read through 1 Timothy 3:1-13 and Titus 1:5-9. These passages were written as a guide for overall church leaders, but they contain much that is relevant for any form of Christian leadership. Discuss with your leaders' team, or pray through yourself, whether the lists raise any problems for you. If so, what can you do about it? Remember that God changes us as we work for him: no one has ever gone into youth leadership (or any other leader's role) as the finished article!

Effective leaders keep growing as Christians. If we're content with the level of discipleship we've reached, the message to group members is that they need not keep striving. If we are constantly being taught, corrected, rebuked and trained in righteousness by the word (2 Timothy 3:16-17) then our members will more easily accept that the same thing needs to happen to them.

Think through the different parts of your body and what they should be like to help you do your youth work well:

listening ears, caring heart, and so on. Pray for help and growth! Obviously, there are many attributes of youth leadership which cannot be linked to particular parts of the body (which is good news for those of us who feel we are less than perfect physically!). Some of these may make us feel very positive: loyalty, sense of humour etc. Others may be more daunting: perhaps self-sacrifice and commitment come into this category.

Commitment

Let's think a little more about that, to be clear about what we're letting ourselves in for. Our commitment will have a major impact on our use of time. We'll have to make sure that enough time is set aside on a regular basis to prepare group sessions, to maintain contact with members outside the sessions and, vitally, to pray.

Our commitment to the young people will also affect our privacy. We don't have to say goodbye to any hope of ever spending a moment on our own. We needn't become a resource that the young people can draw on entirely at will, regardless of our feelings in the matter. Those who go into youth work on that basis soon burn out or give way to massive resentment. However, we'll need to be open and hospitable and we'll sometimes need to let them be with us when we'd rather be doing something else. It's helpful to set clear limits to this, perhaps in terms of one night a week when we will not be available or particular times when we can't be disturbed.

The day after a session on 'Praying and planning for the New Year', a member of the youth group was killed in a car accident. The follow-on pastoral work took months. Emotional detachment in Christian youth work is impossible.

The closer we get to our group members, the more we'll be drawn into their lives, including their emotional ups and downs. Helping them cope will be draining. And our own feelings will not be immune from the effect of working with this volatile, questioning age group. Youth work isn't a question of running a meeting and then going away and forgetting about it until the next one. That's one of the great joys of the job and why it's such an effective way of serving God, but we need to recognize its demands.

What else do we need?

It may help to take other Christian leaders as our role models – without trying to become clones of those people. Who were the people who influenced us when we first followed Jesus? What in their leadership was helpful or attractive? We're all individuals, but we can put those positive things into effect in our own way. Talking of role models, let's be sure to model evangelism with our own peers. It helps us grow, it shows our group that we're serious about what we're telling them to do, and God may save souls by it. Sadly, it's very easy to lose track of our peers when we're focused on the youth work.

One big warning; we always need to beware conceit based on our skills or our status as leaders. Pride has ensnared many Christian leaders and damaged their work. We should remember that Moses, with whom the Lord spoke 'face to face' (Numbers 12:8), was also 'a very humble man' (verse 3). That's a great example for us to measure ourselves against. People will always try to put youth leaders on a pedestal, and we'll be tempted to stay there. The position of leadership that we have, and the skills with which we do it, are given by God and we should be grateful rather than proud about them.

We can develop skills. Our strengths and weaknesses can be balanced by others within a team. We can all pray. If we love God and young people then there's a part for us to play in youth leadership.

INVOLVING GOD

This may sound too obvious to bother with or it may sound like a pious cliché, but it still needs saying: God should be involved. So let's pray. Not now (unless you want to, in which case go ahead and we'll see you in a minute), but constantly about our youth work.

Paul prayed a lot in support of the churches he worked with. He thanked God for them, asked that they would grow in faith, begged that they should be protected from false teaching, longed that their joy in God would increase. It's a great pattern to try to build into our lives. If we can't manage it second by second, at least it is good to pray regularly for our groups. We can pray for people by name, and perhaps base prayer specifically on a passage such as Philippians 1:3-11. And let's pray for our non-Christian members as well, which wasn't Paul's concern when he wrote that passage.

It's good to involve other people in the prayer process. Try to recruit a network of parents, church leaders, friends and the young people themselves. Whether we're starting a new youth work or getting involved in an existing group, the more we can crank up the prayer input, the better.

INVOLVING THE LOCAL CHURCH

The local church should be involved in the group, and the group in the local church. Both of these are easier in some churches than in others, but we need to aim to make both a reality in our youth work.

We must involve the whole church from the outset. Bring the needs of the young people before the whole congregation repeatedly. Suggest that the church puts a figure into its budget for its youth work. Invite adults to participate without necessarily becoming leaders, through prayer and practical help, as occasional speakers, dealing with the money and so on. Talk with the minister about using young people in services, commissioning leaders and so on. We must always have our eyes open to every

way we can involve the young people and adults in each other's lives.

This can be one of the hardest parts of being a youth leader, producing a rich harvest of frustration, guilt and confusion. It's well worth thinking through some strategies for making the necessary links before we plunge into the thick of the work. Useful questions to ponder will include:

● Will I clearly support the minister/church leaders and remain loyal to them within the youth group? This doesn't mean we can never query or disagree with anything they say, but we must accept their authority. It is too easy to allow ourselves to be seen as the cowboy in the white hat, frustrated by the forces of conservatism and fighting a brave battle to free our young people from their shackles.

● Will our group ever discuss (and have biblical teaching on) what it means to be part of the church; locally, world-wide, through history?

● Will we encourage church members to communicate directly with the young people, and not through us all the time?

(The suggested answers to these questions are 'yes', 'yes' and 'yes'. If you answered 'no' to any of them, please

ponder a bit more or give us a call in the CYFA office.)

Keeping the young people and the rest of the church linked prepares the young people for the next stage in their Christian lives. If they are not aware by the time they are 18 or 20 that they are full members of the church fellowship then we won't hold them in that fellowship once they leave our group. Discuss with the minister the church's strategy to hold and help them as they get into jobs, unemployment, marriage and the other aspects of adult life.

(There's more on building bridges between the youth group and the church in Pocket 8.)

POCKET 3

UNDER THE LAW

As responsible youth leaders there are legal and practical issues we will need to think through. They don't need to take up a lot of time as long as they're dealt with sensibly. They are important enough to get right, as ignoring these areas can bring us a lot of problems if something goes wrong. More importantly, it can bring the Church into disrepute.

APPOINTMENT

First of all, it is a good idea for the Church Council formally to appoint the youth leaders. This doesn't need to involve advertising and interviews (though it sometimes will), but the leaders should be accepted by name at a Church Council meeting. This means that there is an official relationship, and the church is seen to take responsibility for its youth leaders. This is important in case of legal problems and also in terms of declaring its support for the work.

INSURANCE

Youth groups need to be insured. In many cases this can be achieved by getting the Church Council to make an extension to its own insurance policy, and this is the simplest way of dealing with the issue. It also means that someone on the Council will probably do the work! If the youth group is an open or ecumenical group it is best to take advice on whose policy will cover the activities. Often the Church Treasurer is the best person to talk to in the first instance.

Failing that, groups from various denominations may find they can link into a scheme run nationally or regionally for youth groups from their own denomination. Possibly, though, we may have to set up a separate policy. In this case, what should be covered?

Legal liability

Legal liability exists where a court would award compensation for injury or damage to property. At least £1,000,000 cover should be provided. Cover will not be provided for certain things such as motor vehicles (a motor policy is needed), boats and so on. If the group uses 'unusual' equipment we'll need to ask the insurer to cover its use specifically. It is unlikely to cost much extra. The policy should include liability of individual leaders and voluntary helpers. This is needed in case someone sues a group leader personally, rather than the church, after an accident.

The insurer may want to know in advance about hazardous activities. This includes obvious things like mountain climbing but also some less obvious things like charity walks. If in doubt, play safe and ring the insurer to check.

Buildings and equipment

The Church Council will have church premises and their contents insured against fire and theft, and perhaps accidental damage. If we meet there we should, therefore, be all right. It is worth checking with whoever handles the insurance arrangements for the church that the normal kinds of activity the group does are covered under those policies – flooding the church hall and freezing it to create an impromptu skating rink might just lie outside the scope of the insurance!

If we meet in premises not belonging to the church we need to check to what extent we are liable for damage. The same applies to using equipment belonging to other people. If we hire or borrow something, whether along the lines of a playing field or a video recorder, for a special event, we may need to ask the insurer to give temporary cover for it. The insurer may well wish to see a copy of a hiring agreement before giving cover.

Additional cover

In addition to the above, it may be worth insuring against:

● loss or damage of personal effects of leaders, voluntary helpers or group members. There will be only limited cover for this and loss of money will probably not be covered. Greater protection is available if people arrange their own insurance.

● loss of money. This means money stolen, not just lost through carelessness. Unless the group is very rich, this is probably not necessary; just be sensible and do not keep significant amounts of cash lying around. Use the church safe or open a bank account.

● group personal accident. This can provide compensation if leaders or group members are killed or injured while taking part in group activities. Again we need to check carefully what circumstances the insurer excludes from cover.

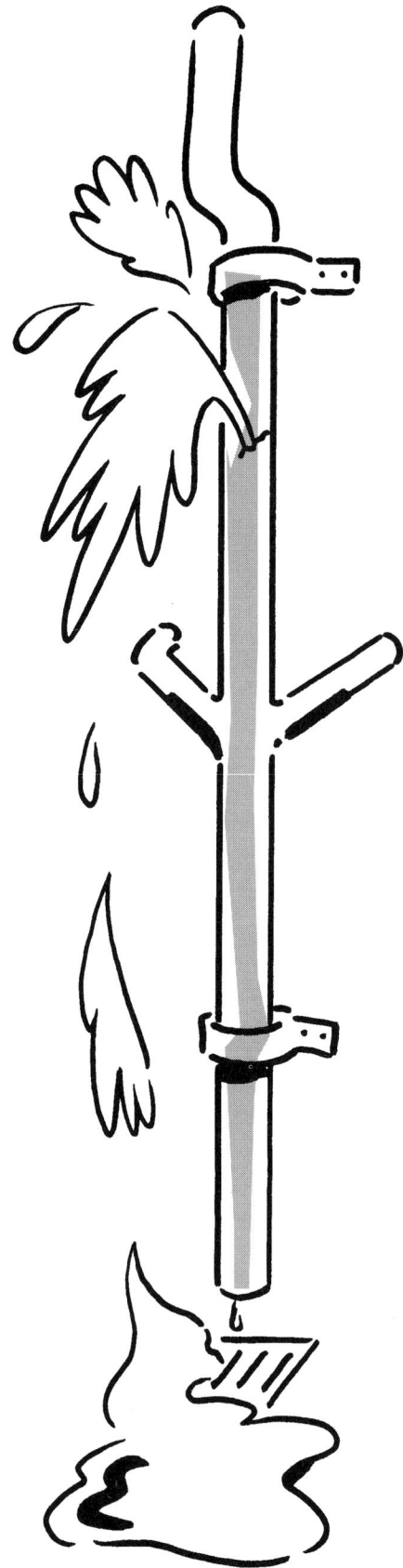

Outings and holidays

If the group goes on an outing or on holiday together, we may need to extend the insurance cover. Equipment used at the church may not be insured for taking elsewhere, nor covered against damage in transit. We may be hiring or borrowing other equipment, or even renting a cottage or other accommodation to stay in. This sort of thing can be added to the insurance temporarily.

If we hire a minibus or other vehicle, we will need motor insurance for that as well. Make sure it includes full third party cover so that passengers' and other people's lives and property are protected. And make sure the driver is legally allowed to drive the minibus, or the insurance may not be valid. If leaders' (or others') cars are used to transport the group, check that their motor insurance will allow this. If necessary, ask the insurers.

As leaders, we may be responsible for group finances, so we may want loss of money cover extended for the duration of the holiday. We will also be responsible for the group members, so check that the legal liability cover includes taking the group away.

Round-up

Obviously the best approach to all these legal and safety questions is to be very careful. Knowing we are insured is not a licence for carelessness. Taking care of people and making sure the practical things run smoothly and safely is one way of showing God's love to them.

For more advice on insurance, talk to an insurance broker (you'll find them in Yellow Pages). The youth officer at the diocesan or other denominational office may well have information about local schemes or regulations – and may even have a block insurance policy for affiliated groups.

Cheer up! Most youth groups never have to make a claim under their insurance policies. Even accidents are thankfully (and surprisingly) rare.

MONEY

If the youth group will deal with money on a regular basis then we need a system for making sure it can be traced and used easily and openly. This is true whether we handle only subscriptions paid by members who come to meetings or we receive a budgeted sum from the church. The first thing is to talk to the Church Treasurer about how best to handle it. If a bank account is needed, it may be best to use one of the existing ones in the name of the church.

With money coming in and going out we will need, at the very least, some record of what is happening and someone to control it. Let's call this person the Banker.

Who should be the Banker? When setting up a youth group from scratch, it may be necessary for the main leader to carry out this function for a while. However, in most other cases it is much more sensible to find someone else. What better opportunity can a leader have to develop responsibility among the members than to entrust the finances of the group to the young people themselves or, failing that, to assistant leaders or helpers?

There is no need for the Banker to have particular qualifications, but he or she needs to feel comfortable with figures and have a thorough approach. This is not the place to go into the practice of book-keeping; suffice it to say that it is not at

all difficult at the level required by most youth groups. The Church Treasurer will be able to explain it quite easily. The following are the main points to watch.

Banking

● Try to find a bank account which doesn't carry charges. Shop around if necessary.

● Make sure that at least two signatures are required on cheques (usually the Banker and any one of two other, named people).

● Reconcile the cash book and bank statements regularly and often.

Records

● Each transaction should be entered promptly in the cash book. Make sure that income and expenditure are clearly identifiable.

● Keep records in an orderly state. Consult the Church Treasurer about how long to keep them.

Income

● Be informed of all income received.

● Ensure that cash is banked regularly.

● If there is a subscription system, make sure it works.

● If refreshments or anything else are sold, ensure maximum security for the funds. At regular intervals check the trading account. Opening stock, plus purchases, less sales should equal the closing stock.

● Think about handing over surplus funds to the Church Treasurer from time to time. Think about giving to Christian work overseas. It is important to liaise with the Church Treasurer here, as in all financial matters.

Expenditure

● All payments made must be properly authorised.

● Always get receipts for expenditure.

● Allow for depreciation and maintenance if the group owns any large equipment.

● Think about contributions to heating and lighting costs for property used.

EVENTS AND PERMISSION

When do we need to get parental permission for the group members to take part in our activities? It depends how much we tell them in advance. If we keep parents/guardians up to date with what the group is doing and what it's for then we'll seldom need to get specific permission. Where we will need to get them to sign something saying they allow their child to take part is:

● When we're doing an activity which involves more than usual risk, like abseiling, sailing, whaling, impaling...For instance, I used to take our group on an overnight walk through the countryside every year. We always had a great time, but we had to cope with livestock, barbed wire, steep bits, darkness. No way would we let anyone come along who didn't bring signed permission from a parent.

● When we're taking the group away from where we normally meet. This may be for a single evening's activity or for a week's holiday. Why not provide parents with a copy of your term's programme and ask them to sign a blanket permission covering the events listed on it? Then they'll have a reminder of what the group is all about, as well.

POCKET 4

WHAT ARE WE TRYING TO ACHIEVE?

What should we be looking for in our youth work? It's all very well knowing what kind of youth leaders we want to be and how to approach the task, but youth work is not an end in itself. We don't do it to make ourselves feel good or so that our church can know that something is happening with the local young people. We do it to get results. So, what do we want to happen as a result of our leadership?

FIRST AND FOREMOST

Our supreme business as Christian youth leaders must be to see conversion and spiritual growth in the lives of our members. Put another way, we want them to start living in relationship with God and then to continue in that way. Sadly, and oddly, we often seem to see the former more than the latter. As we said earlier, we aim with Paul to 'present everyone perfect in Christ' (Colossians 1:28). What does this actually mean? Let's look to the New Testament for some answers and pointers to clarify what we're striving for and some of our methods and motives for achieving it.

What 'potted history' of your Christian life would you give if you were asked? When did you know you were following Jesus? Was it a dramatic moment or a gradual realisation? And what have been the important steps in your continuing growth as God's child?

We'd all come up with different answers, but we all need to be *able* to answer. Thinking about these questions will help you work through the contents of this Pocket, and you'll need to be able to tell the members of your group, too, from time to time.

CONVERSION – CRISIS OR PROCESS?

The New Testament uses many picture words to describe starting the Christian life. Some of these stress what God has done and still does (giving new birth, giving eternal life, convicting us of our sinfulness by his Spirit). Others emphasise our response (believing, receiving or turning to Christ). It is important to notice that all are picture words and that none tells the whole story.

From God's point of view, he is the Creator of all life and by his Spirit he gives new life in Christ. From his viewpoint, a person either is or is not his child. Indeed, in a sense that person has been so from all eternity and will be so for all eternity (Ephesians 1:3-12). So the New Testament is full of very clear distinctions about people. A person is either in Adam or in Christ, in the kingdom of darkness or in the kingdom of God's dear Son, in the world or in the Church.

However, there is also the viewpoint of our human response, of our journeys to faith, and these are as varied as we are. God knows us more intimately than we can imagine. In his infinite love he deals with each of us according to our individual backgrounds (intellectual, sociological and all the rest) and psychological make-ups. The response he wants and draws out must be from the whole person – mind, emotions and will – and these factors are balanced differently in each of us.

It was like this in New Testament times as well. The varied ways in which Jesus dealt with people show this and so do the different paths to faith of Peter and Paul. We can even see in the writings of Paul and John views of salvation which differ in emphasis, though not in the heart of their content.

Paul on the Damascus Road experienced a dramatic confrontation between his former life as an ardent law-keeper and the new grace freely bestowed on the unworthy. He therefore tended to see starting the Christian life as a sudden event; a conclusion reinforced by his experience as an evangelist. For John, who spent three years growing into deeper faith as Jesus' disciple and then probably many years as leader of a church, the stress is different and more gradual. There are shades of belief and the stress is on growing, abiding, feeding and loving, even though he retains the clear-cut distinction of light and darkness.

Ian was brought up with some Bible knowledge and church contact, but no sense that Christianity should have any practical effect on the way he lived. Then at 13 he made a conscious decision to follow Jesus, while on a Pathfinder holiday. The quality of his discipleship fluctuated widely over the next few years, but he could always pin his trust in Jesus as Saviour to that event.

Helen was brought up in a Christian family and absorbed faith, rather taking for granted the truth of what she was taught. She could point to no particular event after which she could say she had become a Christian, but over a period of time in her teens she looked at her faith and made a decision to be committed to it.

Our experience of group members is likely to contain a range of variations of this type. This can cause us and our members difficulties, though it surely causes none to God, who cares that we arrive far more than how we get there! The crisis conversion is exciting and reassuring to look back on. It fits with the emotional peaks and troughs that teenagers experience. This is both an opportunity to be taken, in evangelistic gatherings and Christian holidays, and a danger to avoid. It is easy to use emotionalism, and sometimes it only feeds our need for a visible response. For too many people, only their emotions were converted and years later they look back longingly to a past experience when their present life with Christ should have taken them further. On the other hand the person who has become a Christian gradually may feel they have somehow missed out and look for something dramatic, whether baptism by immersion, confirmation or a pentecostal 'second blessing'. It may be helpful to encourage something along these lines; but it is also vital to point them to the wonder and truth of the Lord's life already within them.

HOW CAN I KNOW IF OTHERS ARE CHRISTIANS?

The fundamental question raised by this fact of differing human responses is: 'How can I know?' How can I know as a leader if someone in my group really is a Christian? Is it so different for each person? Are there any constants? What is the heart of the response that we as leaders look for? We need to ask these questions remembering that in the last analysis only God knows, and only he needs to know, those who are his: the weeds will not be separated from the wheat until Judgment Day (Matthew 13:24-30).

Think of some people who you are confident are Christians. What common factors in their lives give you that confidence?

Three constants reappear in varying guises throughout the New Testament; it is these we should teach and look for.

First, there must be a **death to self**, or **repentance**. This was fundamental in the preaching of Jesus and the early church (Mark 1:15, Acts 2:38, Galatians 2:20). In Dietrich Bonhoeffer's memorable words, 'When Christ calls a man, he bids him come and die'. Hence the biblical stress on turning from idols (Exodus 20:4, 1 Thessalonians 1:9) and the definition of sin as choosing our own way and priorities rather than God's (Romans 1:18-31). However, the 'I' that must die is not the basic personality that God made, but the sinful distortion of it that has taken place. God does not want us all to be the same, but he does want each of us to be the person he intended at our creation and made possible (and, eventually, certain) at our re-creation by his Holy Spirit. Emphasizing this in our groups will mean a much more challenging presentation of the gospel than a simple 'Come to Jesus' – tragically, this often seems to mean no more than 'Add Jesus to your existing life-style'. The cost of discipleship and the radical nature of repentance is an indispensable part of our response to the gospel.

Secondly there must also be clear signs of **a new life begun in Christ**. The first Christian creed was very probably 'Jesus is Lord' (Romans 10:9, 1 Corinthians 12:3). This is significant! Jesus will be the centre and chief delight of any Christian's life. There will be a desire to learn more about him; to spend time with him and his people; a growing realization that he is Lord and therefore I am loved, accepted and safe; but also that I am challenged to make that lordship real in ever new areas of my life and of his world. This newness is not so easy to see when a person has gradually grown into a deepening faith, but the centrality of Jesus is the second inescapable ingredient and is what the New Testament means by 'entering the kingdom', 'believing in Christ' and 'faith'.

Ask your group members to list the five or ten most important people or things in their lives, and to put them in order. Then ask them to work out how long each week they spend on activities associated with each person or item on the list. Is 'God' or 'Jesus' (or 'Bible' or 'prayer' or...) on the list? Does the time allocation match up to the order of priority they put alongside? Don't try to produce guilt or legalism, but do seek realism about the place of God in members' lives. Plan together what they can do as a result.

The third ingredient is **entry into the Church**. Had you asked first century Christians how they knew they were Christians, they would probably have told you of their baptism, so closely linked were being in Christ and being in the Church. So we have verses such as Romans 6:4 and 1 Peter 3:21. Baptism was then the normal way into both Christ and his body, the Church. It vividly portrayed being made one with his death and resurrection. The other distinctive thing the first Christians did together was to break bread.

All this raises questions of our group's links to the local church and the church's attitude to encouraging members into baptism, confirmation and Holy Communion. We'll come back to this topic in Pocket 8.

HOW CAN OUR MEMBERS KNOW THEY ARE CHRISTIANS?

One more question needs answering. If death to self, new life in Christ and church membership are the signs youth leaders can rightly look for in their members to ensure they have started the Christian life, what signs (if any) should we encourage our members to look for in themselves so that they find the assurance of belonging which God longs for them to have (1 John 5:12)? This assurance is a wonderful blessing for our members at the age when they are desperately seeking security and a knowledge that they are loved.

The signs overlap with the previous three and we can deal with them more briefly. First, there will be a **sense of newness**. Christ is the one who makes all things new. Some sense of sin, despair and pointlessness being overcome will be present, though less sharply for the person whose faith has grown gradually. Secondly there will be a **sense of belonging** to the church family, or at least to the youth group. There will be that shared love for Christ, the desire to know him better and to make him better known, and a real hunger for prayer, Scripture and the Holy Communion as the means of grace. It is something of this inner sense that Paul refers to when he says that God's Spirit will witness with our spirit that we are the children of God, finding it natural now to call God 'Abba' or 'dear Father' (Romans 8:15-16). Thirdly, and in many ways most importantly, there are **God's objective promises** of what he has done for each person in Christ. Bible promises such as John 6:37, especially as vividly acted out in baptism (Romans 6:4-5), must be trusted, however an individual may feel at any given time.

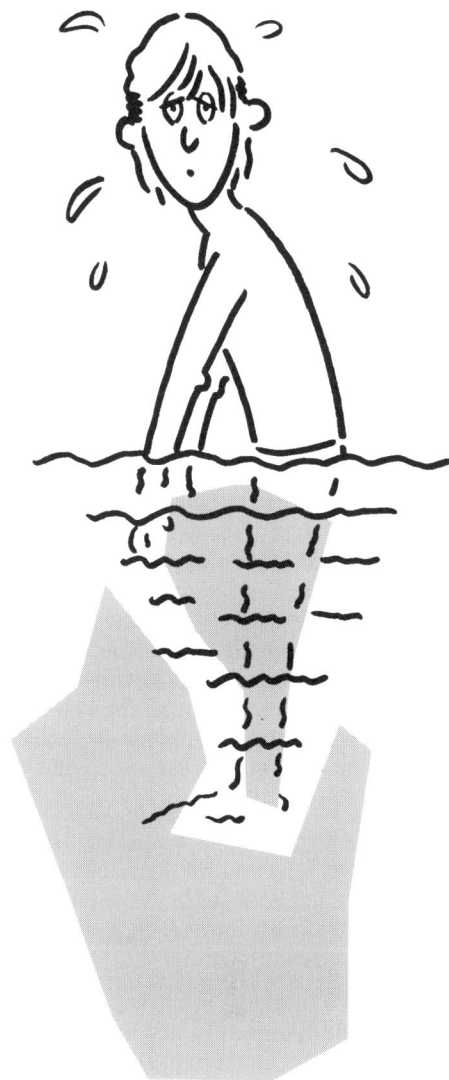

SPIRITUAL GROWTH – CONTINUING THE CHRISTIAN LIFE

It can be sobering to think where our group members will be, as far as the Christian life is concerned, ten or even two years from now. Will they still be church members? Will they have grown spiritually and how can we discern such growth anyway? Growth should presumably be the goal above all others that we work and pray for. Yet it raises questions...

Process or crisis?

Unlike conversion, growth is something in which both the Holy Spirit and the individual play a significant part. God intends us to grow spiritually throughout our lives into Christ's likeness, from one degree of glory to another (2 Corinthians 3:18). The New Testament picture is that with the coming and, especially, the death and resurrection of Jesus, God's rule has broken into our world. The age to come has surged into this evil age. Christians live in both ages while they still overlap, before the age to come replaces this age at Christ's return. This is why Christians still struggle with the old nature, even though the new nature is now within us (Romans 7:14-25). Neither perfect sinlessness nor perfect bodily health are to be found in this life; recipes for instant holiness are a delusion.

However, we are on the victorious side. The more completely we depend on God and the more fully we obey his leading, the more we will experience growth in holiness. In his love, God may well encourage us by some fresh demonstration of his power; this may come as a sudden renewal. Christian growth can therefore be a matter of a sudden great leap forward, though its basic nature and most biblical pictures are those of steady growth.

Sow a seed in a pot. Keep tending it, and use it as a reminder of the importance of growth and the need to pray that our group members' faith will keep growing. If the seed doesn't germinate, pray for those who are showing no growth – and start again with a new seed!

WHAT IS MATURITY?

The basic Old Testament word 'shalom' and a major New Testament concept 'salvation' speak of more than an inner peace with God. The concept is one of wholeness in all of a person's relationships. This includes one's relationship with oneself, but this is not the same as the modern cult of self-fulfilment and independence. Fulfilment is to be found only in Christ, in interdependence with Christ's people and in a relationship to God's world. At an individual level it involves growth in the fruit of the Spirit (Galatians 5:22-23) and a deepening of our understanding of God's truth (Ephesians 4:14-15); that is, moral and doctrinal growth. But it also involves growth in fellowship with other believers and using our different gifts to build one another up (Ephesians 4:11-16). Nor is this simply a church-centred affair. We are saved to serve the needy world. Mission will involve both evangelism and expressing God's desire for more compassion and justice. Above all, maturity involves a deepening of our personal relationship with God, the Three in One. We should echo Paul's longing 'to know Christ' (Philippians 3:10) and to be with him in glory (Philippians 1:21-23).

So, we will be looking for our group to display these characteristics:

● It will be a group whose members love the Lord, feed gladly on his word and use prayer regularly as a means of praise and trust in God. Encourage members to pray in pairs or triplets on a regular basis, sharing answered prayer with the group for encouragement. Be constantly on the lookout for good new Bible study aids to recommend to members whose study is becoming stale.

● It will be an evangelistic group. Too many groups aim only to nurture their current members, without helping them to reach out to their friends and peer group. Include in your teaching sessions from time to time activities which help members identify friends whom they want to see come to the Lord. Arrange social activities which can act as a first step to bringing those people within the sphere of the group. Make sure your members know a brief gospel outline and help them to practise using it.

● It will be a serving group, putting faith into practice in love for God's creation. Approach local nursing homes to see whether the group might be able to visit or help out occasionally. Find a place in your programme for any local initiatives aimed at building the local community. Encourage members to develop a habit of giving money where they cannot give themselves.

● The group will have an outlook wider than its own members or the place where they live, acknowledging that God is Lord of the whole earth and that his people everywhere are our brothers and sisters. Make contact with mission workers who have gone out from your church or elsewhere and get the group to keep up personal contact through letters, phone calls etc. Get in touch with a church (and youth group if there is one) in another country and regularly swap news and prayer requests.

Now, all this is a counsel of perfection. No group shows all these things all of the time. It would be wrong to expect it where some members do not yet know God. But it's a great dream to keep in mind as a guide for our prayers.

HOW IS GROWTH ACHIEVED?

And how is this dream to be realized? Primarily by God, but we need to be aware of the evil one who schemes and fights against us (2 Corinthians 4:4, Ephesians 6:10-11). So we need God's armour; what is called the 'means of grace'. These include prayer, reading the Bible, hearing it expounded and Holy Communion. Much time must be given to enabling our members to benefit to the maximum from these things.

How do we help them? Many of these aspects of growth will be caught from us rather than taught by us. It is striking how Jesus' disciples learned above all simply by being with him and how Paul trained his fellow-leaders by having them with him. He could say to his converts, 'Imitate me' (Philippians 3:17). Time spent with members individually, training given to them as they do things with you and above all the love and prayer that you spend on them are the surest ways to enable God's Spirit to bring them to maturity in Christ.

POCKET 5

'WE WHO TEACH'

Christian youth leaders are Bible teachers. We do much more than teach the Bible, but nothing so important. And it's a huge responsibility (James 3:1). So we must do it well and create the right environment in our meetings for the Bible to do its work. In this Pocket we'll think about what our role as teachers entails, ways of helping people to learn from God's word and how to make best use of our teaching sessions (never forgetting that we teach by example as much as by our words).

THE BALANCE OF THE TEACHING PROGRAMME

We want people to come into peace with God and to stay and grow in that relationship (see Colossians 1:15-23). As this happens, we gradually find peace with ourselves, with others, and with the world at large.

A balanced programme for our group will:

● teach all aspects of this peace from the Bible

● allow group members to encounter expressions of these aspects in the group

● encourage group members to commit their lives to Christ

● train group members in the skills and godly attitudes they may need in any area of life.

This means that the teaching programme will provide a mixture of doctrine, application to everyday life and challenges to commitment and growth. It is important not to concentrate exclusively on any one area. Looking only at doctrine produces head-knowledge without skill in putting it into practice; our aim is not to produce members who are good at biblical Trivial Pursuit. Looking only at 'real-life issues' means that the world sets our agenda. An evangelistic challenge every week blunts its impact and tempts members to say what we want to hear, just to get over that routine part of the meeting.

HOW PEOPLE LEARN

There are as many different learning styles as there are people, but it's possible to identify some broad categories which describe how most of us learn. Some of these are easier to use when following up a teaching session than in the session itself, but we can use them all. This means that everyone will find something which suits them. Trying to fit all the styles into one session is messy and frustrating; it's best to vary what we do from week to week, so that we don't ignore any one style for too long.

Four learning styles

Some people need to see an example

Abstract concepts may mean very little to such people, but a case study or a character study from the Bible can open things up for them and help them to see how a principle applies in their own lives.

Some people need to do

Projects or practical work, following up teaching points, can be a key way of learning for these people. Demonstrations and practical exercises are very helpful within teaching sessions, and to get the young person involved in preparing and presenting the session is a great help.

Some people need to analyse

Asking 'why?' and working out the reasons behind things is crucial for these learners. They will need space to ask questions and to work things out for themselves. 'Real-life' examples are of less help (and interest) than underlying concepts.

Some people need to weigh things up

Just mulling over what they've heard, read or seen is essential for this group. They won't come up with quick answers or decisions – or, if they do, it may be only to keep us happy. Feed these people information and experience and they will work through it in their own time.

Which learning style described here is nearest to your own? Think of something you have learnt recently. What made it easy or difficult to learn? What might have made it easier for someone with a different learning style?

TEACHING THE BIBLE

So much of the problem that young people have in getting to grips with the Bible is their feeling that it is too big and too out of date to be worth bothering with.

Dealing with the bigness of the Bible

We can show the group that the Bible is a collection of different books rather than one item which has to be digested in a single gulp. (Of course, we need to be able to show how the whole thing hangs together, but that's another issue.) Use games like the ones mentioned later in this Pocket to familiarise them with individual Bible books. Simply being able to say whether a book is in the Old or New Testament can do surprising things for a teenager's confidence in approaching the Bible.

The next level might be to look at the different types of writing in the Bible: history, prophecy, law, gospels, apocalyptic, pastoral, wisdom. Bring in a cake with several different layers to your meeting, and use it to illustrate how the different types of writing go to make up the whole. Eat the cake together. It's memorable and it meets the Christian youth group's need for constant food.

When teaching, consider typing out the passage onto A4 and photocopying. It saves members feeling swamped by a 1300-page book.

Dealing with the oldness of the Bible

First of all, the young people need versions of the Bible which they can understand. If that means a translation which seems ridiculously basic, so be it. They can always graduate to something more challenging and accurate later on. If they're 'not bookish' we can help them to understand it. It is not a condition of membership, either of the group or of heaven, that they should love to read. Still, we are a people whose faith is based on what we read in a book, so don't be soft about the need to feed on the Bible. Play tapes of people reading passages, use dramatized versions and do whatever it takes to convince the members that the Bible can be understood today, but keep it in front of them as an essential for anyone seeking to follow Christ. They can grow into it, but they can't grow without it.

Three keys

So how do we entice young people to explore God's word? Three key concepts to keep in mind are involvement, relevance and application.

Involvement means getting the young people to experience the passage with as many of their senses as is possible without things getting farcical, and also with their emotions. Hearing a passage read may be for many of them like listening to football results on the radio. Seeing a dramatized version may be like watching a game. We need to try to give them something like the experience of playing in a match. (This part of the book was written during the Euro '96 football tournament. Non-football fans please write rude comments at the bottom of the page and then apply the principle to one of your own favourite activities.) So let's use visual aids and sound effects, give parts to group members to act out, build games and pauses for thought into our Bible passages, and do everything we can to build involvement.

Failure to see the **relevance** of the Bible is perhaps the biggest stumbling block of all for young people in coming to know and love God and his word. Our members need the chance to ask questions about how events and teachings from so long ago still affect us now – whether in our personal lives or in the world around us. God is still God; 'Jesus Christ is the same yesterday and today and for ever' (Hebrews 13:8). So his word is bound still to be relevant, and our job is to show our group how that is true.

As for **applying** the Bible to their lives, if our young people don't do that then no amount of head knowledge about the Bible and its relevance will be any use to them. In our teaching we need to lead them to the answers to both 'What does the Bible say?' and 'What does this mean for me?' Answering only the first question will leave them dry and unsatisfied; answering only the second can lead to all sorts of unbalanced and self-centred beliefs.

So we want to feed the minds, hearts, emotions, and wills of our young people when we look at the Bible with them. On the next page are some ideas, old and new, bookish and otherwise, for ways in which to do that.

GIVING A TALK

Please remember that giving a talk is not the only way to teach young people. Nor is it the most important or effective, though it is important and effective if well done and mixed with other teaching methods. However, since it causes fear and grief for many group leaders, we will spend a few moments here thinking about how to do it well.

Do

● Use talks and mini-talks as part of your teaching. They're not out of date and they don't have to be boring. Jesus spent a lot of time giving talks (there's not a lot of active learning in the Sermon on the Mount).

● Have a structure: introduce what you're going to say, give your main input and then summarise briefly to help people remember what they've heard.

● Make sure you're well prepared. If you don't really know what you're talking about then we all end up thinking that talks are a bad way of using our time.

● Vary your tone and the pace of what you're saying. When you listen to good speakers, try to think how they keep your attention. But don't let their expertise intimidate you; they had to start from scratch as well!

● Illustrate what you're saying. Anecdotes, examples, visual aids and activities all add to the impact.

● Go through what you're planning to say with someone else beforehand, and have them give you some feedback afterwards (but not straight away – give yourself time to wind down).

(See page 24 for what **not** to do in a talk)

OPENING UP THE BIBLE

1. Swedish Bible study. Nothing to do with flogging yourself with birch twigs and rolling in the snow, although you can if you want to as long as you have parental permission. Give each group member a sheet of paper with a candle, an arrow and a question mark drawn on it. As you look at the passage, they make a note against the candle for any verses which shed light on something for them; against the arrow for any verses which challenge them or prick their conscience; and against the question mark for any verses which they don't understand. Use the completed sheets as a basis for discussion. (There are all sorts of variations on this idea – develop your own to suit your group.)

2. Little Bible. Have the names of all the books in the Bible printed on individual slips of paper. If your group has little Bible knowledge, just add a few decoys and challenge them to pick the real from the false, moving on to split them into Old and New Testament and to give one or two facts about the books they have on their slips. A group with good Bible knowledge can be split into small teams, which have to barter for books to get the 'best' Bible they can if they're allowed only, say, twelve books each.

3. Re-creation. Write each verse from a passage on individual slips of paper and get members to put the passage together again, having heard it earlier in the meeting. This is easier with narrative than with, say, Psalms or Proverbs.

4. SFX. Get small groups to retell a Bible story using only sound effects. Things like the fall of Jericho and the feeding of the 5,000 are good starting points.

5. Detectives. Produce evidence and ask members to deduce what the story is. For example, use a white stick and dark glasses for the healing of a blind man. Use this method, too, to ask what sort of problems the churches had that Paul's letters addressed. Use a concordance to help members find out about lesser-known Bible characters.

6. Rewrites. The group rewrites the passage in the style of various magazines and newspapers that you have available. Things like the *Just 17* version of David and Bathsheba can be particularly memorable.

7. Character following. Allocate characters from the passage to members of the group. Ask them to consider their characters' feelings and reactions.

8. What happened next? Take a passage that is not too well known. Read it a section at a time and ask what happened next. Give multiple choice answers to get things moving.

9. Headings. Type out passages without the headings given in your Bible version. Ask members to give each section a heading. Share results.

10. Editing. Give members a 200-word passage and ask them to edit it down to 100, then 50, then 25, then 1.

Don't

● Try to include too much. Be realistic about how much people can cope with, in terms of concentration span and the number of points they can remember from a session.

● Read a script. You're giving a talk, not a reading. By all means use notes – very full notes if that gives you more confidence – but know them well enough to be able to look up from time to time and make eye contact with the group.

So, we combine different ways of teaching and remember that the most important thing is how much the group takes in. That's down to their styles of learning and the relationship we have with them as much as our technical skills. There are plenty of resources around, produced by CPAS and other organizations, which can help with the basic input on any number of topics.

WHAT ABOUT THOSE WACKY ACTIVITIES?

One group had a Bible study on one of the two stories of the talents (Matthew 25:14-30 and Luke 19:11-27). It was the story where each received different amounts, but the group ended up blending the two by handing out to each member one gold coin (£1) about a month before the summer fair and telling them to trade with it.

Some made cakes or jam to sell, one made children's aprons, another bought a leather and washed cars. With the proceeds of sales and work even before the fair, they were able to buy more ingredients and so make more money. At the fair sixteen people ended up making over £100. And that was just the extended visual aid!

In organizing activities for youth groups, we must be prepared to think creatively and try things out. We have to allow ourselves to be fools, if necessary, to serve others and demonstrate that Christian teenagers can enjoy something of life in all its fullness (John 10:10). We need to be bold in choosing and trying out ideas. Young people want things to go well but they often don't know how to make or help it happen. They may lack the social confidence to try but they will follow a clear, confident and cheerful lead into even the most outrageous activities and initiatives.

So let's have big and unusual ideas, and experiment. Let's think things through beforehand, then launch them with panache and expect others to follow. No one in their right mind normally wants to get wet but if it is assumed that all will take part in trying to catch water-filled balloons (which everyone knows are completely unpredictable as to when and over whom they burst) then the crowd will all try it, most will get soaked and everyone will love it.

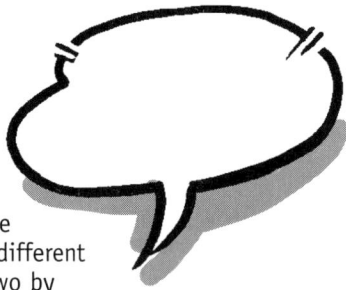

Plagiarize and improvize

Plagiarize relentlessly, from Christian and non-Christian sources. If we can't out-think the world, we can still borrow its ideas and adapt them to Christian ways. There are lots of books of games and activities, and most ideas can be reshaped if they're not right to start with. We can wander round shops and see what games can be reconstructed for our groups. We can lift ideas from the television.

You come across six discarded cardboard tubes from carpet rolls. They are each eight feet long. It would be a pity to waste them; so what could you devise?

Improvize with materials and within activities as you go along. You'll astonish yourself. The key is to be interested. Be curious to learn and see and try things for yourself. It's a great boon if you're really only leading others into what you love doing yourself.

STRUCTURING A SESSION

There is no 'right' way to put together a teaching session. Variables like the time and resources available and the stage the group is at will affect what we include and in what order.

As basic guidelines we could say:

● All the different elements of the session should have some connection with the theme, to reinforce the learning point, unless you are deliberately trying to keep people guessing.

● Provide a space within the session for the group to consider their response to what they have heard, seen or done.

● Recap from time to time on what has already happened in the session.

● Balance lively and quieter activities and use them to produce the appropriate atmosphere for what is coming next. Try to have extra activities up your sleeve so that you can substitute a more appropriate one if the atmosphere is drifting away from what you want.

● Most importantly, know what the focal point of your meeting is, and make the other elements serve that purpose. Sometimes you may focus on building the group, sometimes you may want to focus on praising God, sometimes (often, we hope!) on helping the members apply Bible truths to their lives. Time given to other activities and topics will vary accordingly.

WORSHIP

Worship is about giving back to God what he is worth. We just can't do it, but the Bible encourages us to do the best we can. This involves the whole of our lives, and particularly the ways in which we serve God, and not just our 'praise' activities. More than one Greek word in the New Testament is translated 'worship' in our Bible versions, and if you look at the idea of 'worship' with your group then a word study would be a good thing to include.

When you and your group want to praise God, you may find singing difficult for various reasons:

● nobody can play an instrument

● their voices are breaking and they're embarrassed

● there are too few of them.

If these things are not a problem then there are masses of Christian songbooks around these days and you will be able to find something that suits your group. Your members may have their favourites from church or perhaps from Ventures, camps and houseparties.

If the things mentioned above are a problem for your group, there's no need to worry – singing is not the only way a group can worship God. You could gain great benefit from:

● buying appropriate resources from the booklist at the end of this book

● doing something other than singing; try silence, meditation, spoken words of praise, dance and/or listening to one of the many CDs or tapes that are available

● inviting the young people to consider their response to God and to create their own worship. This is how much of today's alternative worship scene developed.

The key thing is to focus on God in a way which engages the commitment of the young people. We're trying to come close to God and strengthen the body of Christ, so anything which works towards those aims is worth trying. Let their imaginations have free rein. Let them speak out. It is worth thinking about the words of Job's young friend Elihu, who almost bursts with frustration as he waits for the adults to finish before he speaks (Job 32:6-20).

Sometimes, though, young people's reluctance to get involved in 'worship' is not a product of frustrated creativity but of ignorance of the Lord. If they are completely set against taking part in praise of any sort, don't force it; it will only reinforce their dislike. There is nothing magic or obligatory about having a 'worship slot' in each meeting. Give it a rest (but keep the issue on the agenda) and pray that their hearts will be warmed so that they feel the need to respond to God. And be prepared with ideas to help them when they reach that state.

WHAT'S GOING ON?

Publicizing the group's activities well can make the difference between sporadic attendance and a more loyal core, eager to see what happens next. Not only can advance knowledge of the programme reassure group members and their friends that the group's agenda is something they need and will enjoy, but producing the publicity can be a great activity to involve the group in. Use their gifts! Here are some ideas for producing something to catch the eye and the attention without getting involved in a time-consuming heap of work.

If we want to produce effective publicity, we need to relate it to the world our young people are living in. To do this we must understand the graphic language they are familiar with; we may need to do a little research into the graphic design that teenagers are surrounded by and feel comfortable with.

Buy a few copies of teenage magazines (*Smash Hits, Just 17, Kerrang!* and so on). They'll give an insight into the culture that many young people are in contact with. Look at how the articles are presented and how the design is or isn't linked to the titles. Also, pop into Top Shop, River Island and Miss Selfridge and see how graphics are used to promote the clothes. Look at the sleeves on new music releases. All these things are part of the 'graphic language' that our young people are used to.

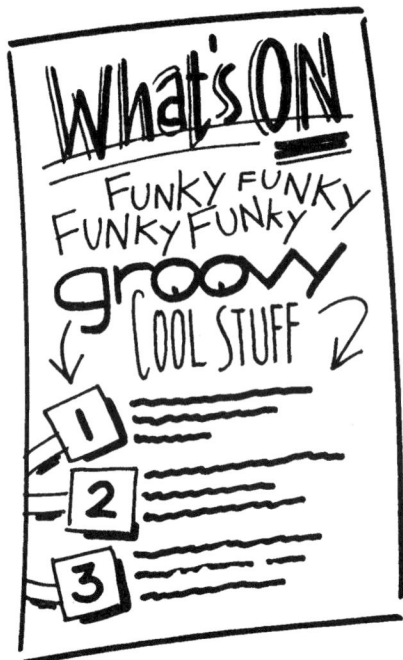

The next thing to consider is what format to use. Many programmes are A4 (the size of this page) or A5 (half that size). Producing cards this size is easy, but by all means try something more unusual.

Even working on an A4 sheet we can cut it to produce two triangular programmes. Some groups use several sheets of paper and produce a quarterly youth group magazine.

Another important aspect to consider is colour. In the magazines it is obvious that colour plays an important role. We can use colour effectively and cheaply in a number of ways: print on coloured paper; print or photocopy in a single colour; spice up the finished result by adding self-adhesive, coloured stickers. Research shows that people respond more positively to colour advertisements, so it's wise to include colour somewhere in our publicity material. Full-colour photocopiers exist, but are very expensive.

Do use pictures and other graphic material in the programme. They break up the page, add interest, emphasise points and can inject humour. Use group members' illustrations, photographs, copyright-free clip art or anything else you can find. Remember the limitations of your method of production – dark

colour photographs will not reproduce well on navy blue card!

Try to collect programmes from other groups, to see how other people are doing it. A good programme card can be a very useful tool in building momentum into a series of meetings and events. It will not, of course, make up for a poor programme. Decide the content of the teaching and social programme before thinking about the printed back-up material, and make sure the material serves the work rather than dictating its direction.

Having done the preparation, now is the time to decide on design. Sit down with a pencil and sketch out some ideas; or get the group to do it. Look out for members with artistic or creative talents, including being able to write the words. Last comes physically putting the programme together. Hand-written programmes tend to look messy and unappealing (unless calligraphy is a gift we can access), so use Letraset, text cut out of publications, or typed material. Most churches now will include people with computers which have a range of typestyles, and they may be able to produce pictures as well. Ask around. It's another good way of getting more people involved with the youth work.

DICTATORSHIP OR DEMOCRACY?

Who is going to decide what goes on the programme, when meetings happen, where to go for outings and all the other details of group life? Some of us love being in control and will immediately fill any leadership vacuum. Others prefer to let other people take the decisions.

If the bulk of the decisions are going to be made by the leadership team, it is important that the members have a chance to make some input into the process. After all, if we're trying to help them towards maturity we can't treat them like little children. So we may have a structured forum where they can feed us ideas, or we may just take informal soundings as to what they think should happen. With this informal model it's important that everybody feels part of the process, rather than that a small 'inner core' is claiming to speak for everybody.

Such a core can, however, be valid if it is a recognized group such as a committee, chosen by the rest of the young people. This arrangement means they must be committed and the group must trust them, and not all groups at all times can achieve these things. However, with proper encouragement it can call forth unexpected abilities and maturity. Clearly the scope of the committee needs to be plainly stated; there will be some things which group leaders and other church leaders will need to reserve for their own decision. The keys to helping a committee to work well are to offer support if wanted, to resist any inclination to take back things you have handed over to them and to pray for them.

SYLLABUSES – PLANNING OUR TEACHING

Our aim with our teaching sessions should be to provide systematic learning over the weeks, months and years: not giving undue weight to our favourite topics nor avoiding those we're uncomfortable with, but helping our young people to explore 'the whole will of God' (Acts 20:27). What should we aim for?

We ought to be presenting a fully-rounded, balanced and lively programme of worship and learning. Hopefully this is also what our church will be doing, and sometimes we will be able usefully to link the programmes together.

We need variety of presentation (not all talks, all videos or all discussion) as well as variety of content.

Some topics, such as prayer, are basic and will require repetition.

It is a good idea to have fairly regular 'special' meetings, perhaps with outside speakers or with a practical focus so that the group does things together as well as learning together. Putting some aspect of what has been learnt into practice by serving others would fall into this category.

It's also good, and even essential, to take the group away for weekends or longer periods. CPAS and other organizations run holidays with teaching and activities, or we can do our own thing. What are the advantages? Well, for a start people often feel able to relax and open up when they get away from their usual surroundings. Doing different activities may lead to opportunities to talk which may be hard to come by in the normal routine of the work. And trips away can be really useful in topping up the fun factor which is so important for keeping an edge on work with teenagers. Even travelling to the venue can be as much fun and as good for building relationships as the time away itself.

Just think: If we spend an hour a week with our group, it will take half a year to spend a day with them. Spending residential time with them means we achieve that day's contact in, oddly enough, a day.

How to get started

First and most obvious and basic, we pray! We seek wisdom in assessing how far we are covering a balanced selection of his truth and how effectively we are communicating it. And we ask God also to show us the current spiritual needs of the group.

What has been covered in past 'programmes'? Check for significant omissions or imbalances. Try to remember the methods of presentation used and see whether the same method has been used very often. Think about

talks, slides, tapes, videos, drama, interviews, discussions, Bible study, games and so on. If there are no records of what's been covered in the past, let's start keeping them now!

Then we can think, pray and chat with older Christians about what to do. Do our members need spiritual milk or meat? Most subjects can be taught even to young Christians, so we don't always have to go at the speed of the slowest. A steady flow of new members will probably require a basics course each year – perhaps this should take place at a different time from the main meetings. It is sometimes a good idea to give members a questionnaire to assess what they have enjoyed most up till now and what they think they need next. This will also help to show us what the members are learning elsewhere. No group ought to exist in isolation. They may learn at church, in basics courses, at school CUs, or in home groups. Let's rejoice in the help this gives us!

THE HUMAN FACTOR

FAMILIES

The Bible does not allow us to consider young people apart from their families. We must take our responsibility to families seriously (for example, evening meetings and activities should end punctually). It may help to visit parents or guardians with a card, giving an outline of the usual programme and details of the adults responsible for their children when they are at the youth group.

Non-church families are a natural (and often neglected) opening for evangelism, and an aspect of youth work which is often forgotten is that it is possible to have some very useful contacts with parents. It can be a way in to challenging parents about their own faith, or lack of it.

However, there are dangers to be aware of:

● making the group members feel that they are just tools that we're using to achieve a hidden agenda of reaching their parents

● antagonizing parents so that their attitudes against the church are hardened, which may also lead them to give their children problems over attending the group

● transferring our feelings about group members onto their parents, and vice versa. They are all individuals in their own right, and it is wrong to treat members in a particular way because of how we perceive their parents.

One other point to bear in mind with regard to parents is that we need to keep up to date about the home lives of our members, and to use that information sensitively. It is all too easy to make assumptions in our teaching sessions and discussions about the presence at home of parents, or about the way they treat their children. We don't want to be always digging for hidden traumas, but we do need to avoid generalizations which can hurt and alienate the young people we're working with.

YOUNG PEOPLE FROM CHRISTIAN FAMILIES

There are problems to be faced by most young people who grow up in a Christian family. Their family is different from most and there's a stigma attached to this. We must remember this because it can become the driving force in a young person's life.

This doesn't mean that Christian families should not stand out and be different, nor that their children will be disadvantaged if they do so. Problems can mature the personality, and throughout the Bible God's people are called to be different. But we need to watch that our teenagers deal with the problems in healthy ways. They will be intensely conscious of their peers and they're likely to have more difficulties with the stigma now than at any later stage. Indeed, the way they manage it now may well decide whether they continue into adult life as Christians or abandon the faith.

At any time our youth group will probably contain a variety of young people who have adopted very different strategies for coping. Let's look briefly at five major ones.

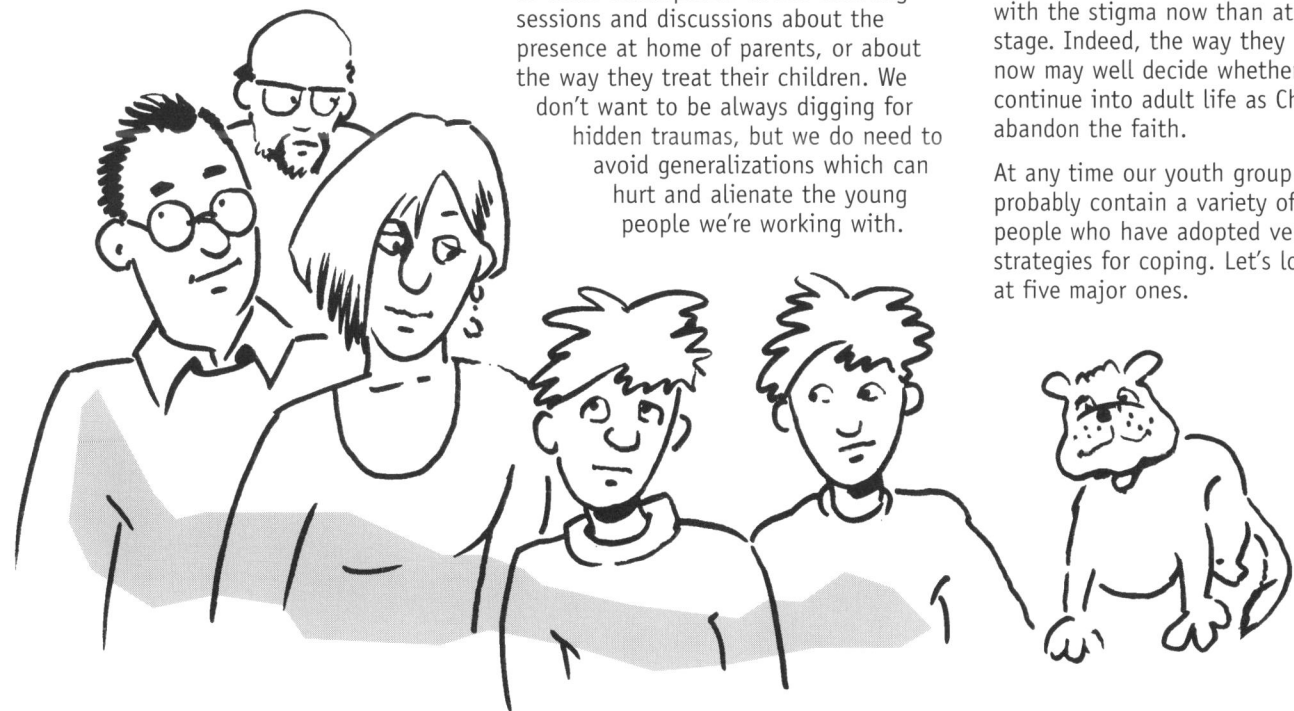

Rejection

To some young people, being accepted matters so much that they react against their 'abnormal' background and try desperately to prove that they are just like 'normal' teenagers. This can be violent rebellion – open refusal to live up to the hopes of their parents – or covert behaviour, outwardly doing and saying the right things while living a double life on the quiet.

Young people may adopt this course because they don't understand why Christians are supposed to be different. There is then no reason for them to behave in ways which highlight a gap between them and most of their friends.

The second main reason why young people reject their background in favour of esteem from their peer group is because they don't receive the esteem they crave from their parents. Christian parents are often very protective and yet ready to find fault with their children, even when they have a very real and deep love for them. This can create a sense of lack of worth. As youth leaders we have a chance – albeit temporary and limited – to supply some of the missing sense of worth. We can give responsibility and trust, and can show that we value the young person as an individual with a unique contribution to make.

Fake super-spirituality

Another 'false front' adopted by many is the attitude that reasons, 'Well, if I've got to look unusual in front of my peers, I may as well look really unusual. I'm going to stick out like a sore thumb anyway, so let's make a virtue out of necessity.' Super-keen Christianity becomes the sense of identity for such teenagers. If they stick it out for a while they know they will be accepted in that role – thought a bit odd but no longer laughed at since their behaviour is perfectly consistent. There will even be grudging respect for people so sure of their beliefs. It's not popularity, but it's acceptance.

Of course, spiritual enthusiasm among teenagers doesn't always have this motivation. Still, the zeal shown by a Christian teenager is sometimes not so much evidence of deep security in Jesus as a cover for a gnawing insecurity. Such people will often fall away completely later. Praise God, though, it is possible for people wearing such a mask to mature into well balanced Christian adults. What can we do to help? (Apart from praying, of course, which is the most basic and important thing to do for any of our group members.)

One important principle is not to take them too seriously. We can show that we love and value them without joining in the chorus of uncritical praise they will tend to attract. If we challenge glib statements and slack thinking, they may become hostile. If this happens, we stay committed to them and let them know how much we value them as people rather than performers. In the end they will realize they can trust our honest reactions.

We can also help by exposing people to new needs. It is hard to keep up the act of being a Christian super-hero when your faith is battling with new challenges. Cosy, uncritical, self-admiring youth groups don't provide this challenge, so our groups must not become like this. And we must challenge people to express their Christian zeal in service to others. If our teenagers define 'spirituality' as listening to the latest worship tapes or going to lots of meetings, they can easily coast along. If we teach them to think of it in terms of looking after widows and orphans in their distress, we're more likely to end up with pure and faultless religion (James 1:27).

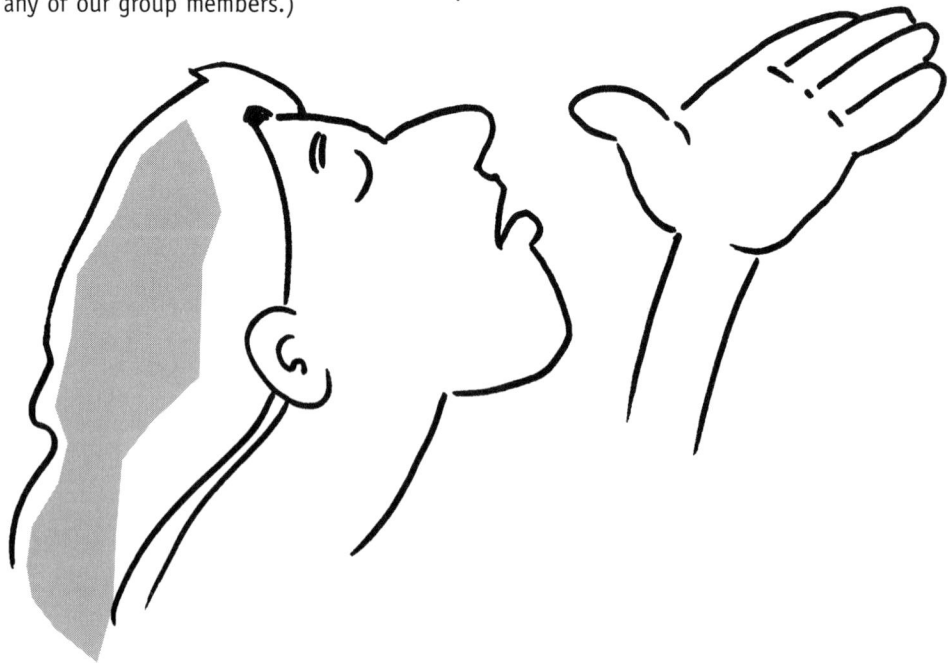

The clown

Some young people find that a good way of compensating for a social disadvantage – like 'being religious' – is to make people laugh. And of course humour can be a tremendous aid to recommending the gospel. But wise youth leaders will scrutinize the local clowns with care. All too often, comedians are the most desperate human beings: many have ended up killing themselves or with wrecked lives.

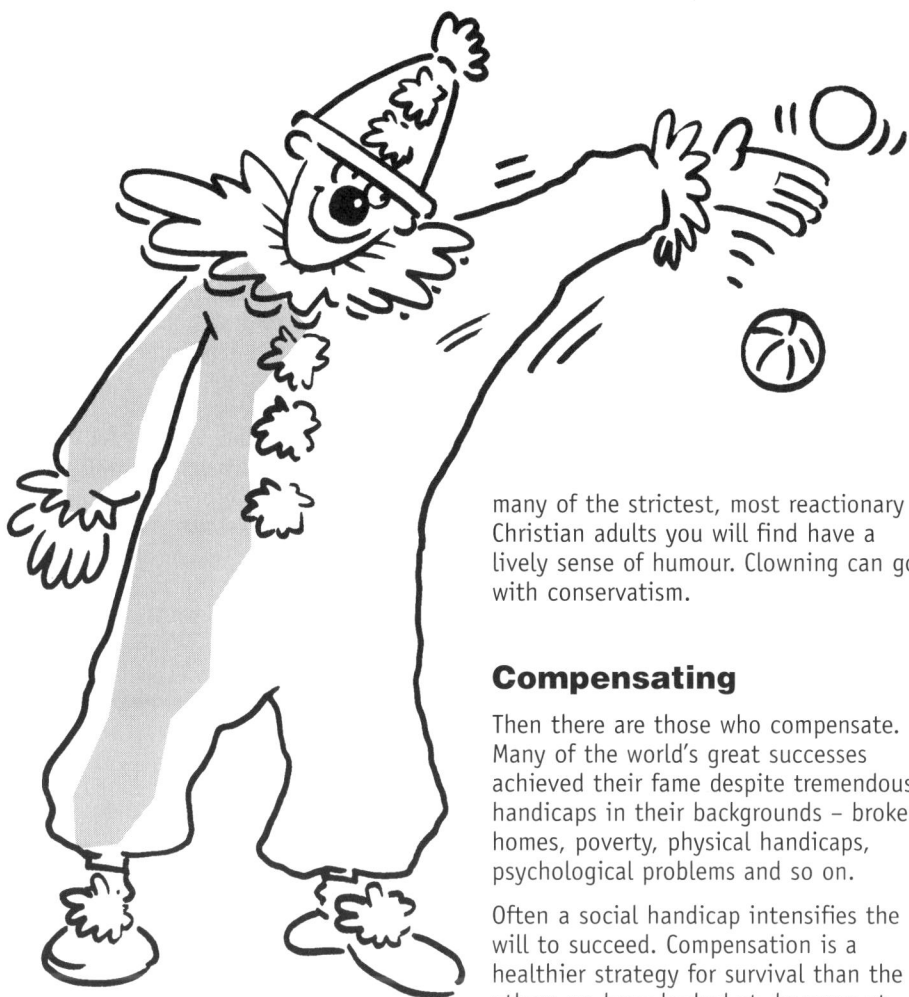

Humour, especially wry, self-directed humour, can be a way of making the best of inferiority feelings: a second-rate technique of survival which takes the place of openly examining these feelings and dealing with them. Laughing about it all can be a way of evading serious questions – Do I really believe this stuff? Is it really true? – and making life comfortable enough to avoid the agony of facing change. Clowns in youth groups tend not to be the most progressive, dedicated members; and many of the strictest, most reactionary Christian adults you will find have a lively sense of humour. Clowning can go with conservatism.

Compensating

Then there are those who compensate. Many of the world's great successes achieved their fame despite tremendous handicaps in their backgrounds – broken homes, poverty, physical handicaps, psychological problems and so on.

Often a social handicap intensifies the will to succeed. Compensation is a healthier strategy for survival than the others we have looked at, because at least it is positive. It means standing out against pressures rather than allowing oneself to be moulded by them, which is what all the other strategies have really been about. But the compensation activity (whether it's doing well at school, becoming a super-athlete, gaining a reputation for computer wizardry, or whatever) can start to assume an emotional importance of its own which we must look out for.

It is all too possible for talented young people to pour all their efforts into succeeding in their chosen way, remaining content with a very superficial Christian experience. Compensating helps survival as a Christian, but not growth. The two separate worlds need to be brought together somehow.

Caving in

Finally, there are the young people who cave in. They give up trying to be different: their parents would not allow it anyway. So they turn into pocket-sized versions of what their parents were twenty years before, and retreat within themselves, timidly living predetermined lives. There are more of these in Christian circles than we like to pretend.

How can we help these young people? It is never easy; they deliberately shut themselves away inside, masking all traces of individuality because independent thinking has always meant trouble. We must help them gradually to regain confidence in their own worth as human beings – by giving them tasks they can do and gradually trusting them with more responsibility. They will resist this, because they have chosen the path of leaving responsibility to others; but often when they do something right, and realize it, and become aware that the youth leader values them as individuals, there can be a slow and cautious blossoming of the personality which is very satisfying to see.

Just to plunge people like this into strange, unprecedented experiences will make them shrink deeper and deeper into their shell. We need to do it slowly, gently broadening their horizons; never taking them on further than they are ready for; waiting till they feel comfortable with one set of new perceptions before we confront them with another. It's sad that it should take so much time and patience to undo some of the harm which Christian parents have done to their children. But it needs to happen.

And so...

Rejection, over-enthusiasm, clowning, compensation, caving in – all are ways of staying afloat. But all have their dangers and some are downright unhealthy. We don't want our young people just to 'stay afloat'. We want them to grow into confident, full-blooded, heartfelt commitment to Jesus Christ, and healthy, mature adult living as a result. Perhaps in all this the key word is 'balance'. That applies to our youth work, too: Christian parents can try to steer it in excessively 'safe' directions and we'll need to deal wisely with that.

OURSELVES

In considering the human factors involved in youth work, let's not forget ourselves (if there are any dogs or albatrosses reading this, you are extremely clever and should go into show-business, but the book is intended for humans).

Under the constant pressure of feeding and loving our members, let's remember that our own spiritual health is an important factor in how well we do that work. We can't keep on giving to others if we are not receiving from God. So, what are the key components which keep us healthy in our spiritual walk?

First comes the Bible. It is all too easy for us to fall into the trap of treating God's word as merely the raw material for our group sessions, rather than something we need to read and apply to ourselves for our own sakes. A quick dip into a gospel on a Sunday afternoon to dig out some references for that night's session will not keep us refreshed and responsive to the Father. We exhort our young people to be disciplined in regular study and to apply to their lives what they read. They will see how we ourselves treat and use the Bible, and the odds are that they will mirror what we do more than what we say. So for our sakes and for theirs, let's have a right approach to God's word.

Then, too, we need to be conscientious in prayer. That may sound a bit dry; it would be better if we could just float along joyfully on a tide of prayer. And sometimes that may be the case. But life is tough, we get tired, and it's more important to keep praying than to feel good about it. We need to step aside from activity, to keep contact with the Father and to make sure that we bring all of our life under his watchful and willing eye.

We should also be sure to play a full and regular part as members of our own church. This does not mean taking on more and more responsibilities; it means being fed, being cared for, being part of a body. We need to receive as well as give.

Balancing our time between the group and our family is an important issue which we need to keep under constant review. Obviously the extent of family commitments differs widely for different leaders, but very few of us are completely without ties. God loves it when we do our youth work well; he also takes family responsibility with the utmost seriousness (see, for example, 1 Timothy 5:8). Taking regular stock of how we're doing in this regard, and talking it through honestly with those who are affected, is very important. It is all too easy to bask in a glow of pleasure about how well we're doing (and how self-sacrificial we're being) in our youth work, while in the background tensions and resentments build up on the family scene which will bear destructive fruit later on.

As we think of our own spiritual walk, it is helpful to think of ourselves as pilgrims on a journey; progressing, but not there yet! One of the many uses of this picture in the Bible is in Psalm 84:5-7. Read these verses through and see how those on the journey are themselves blessed by God, while acting as a source of blessing to their surroundings – a very good image for youth leaders to aspire to.

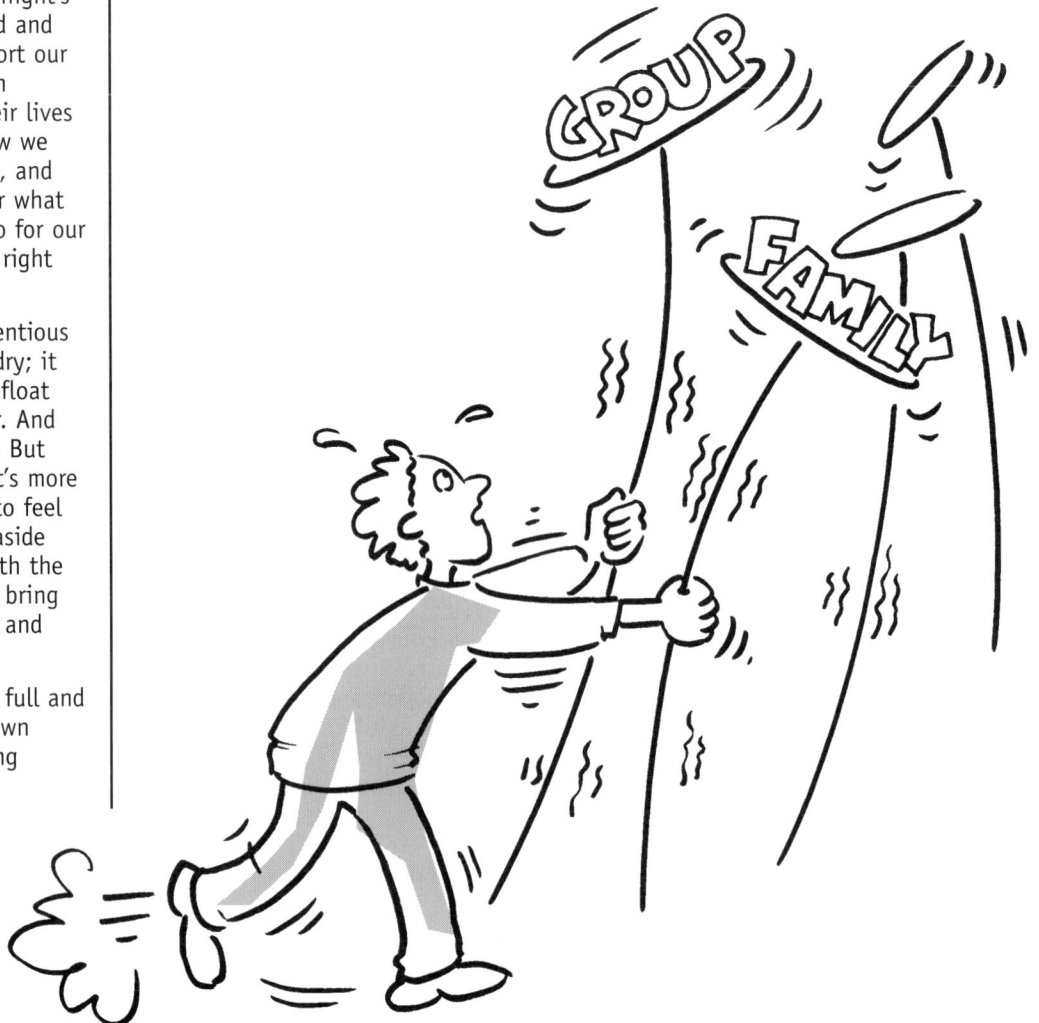

POCKET 7

THE ROUGH WITH THE SMOOTH

COMMON-SENSE COUNSELLING

Youth workers are not counsellors unless they are specifically and properly trained in counselling. However, all youth workers need a few, basic counselling skills because young people are people and people have problems. Sometimes teenagers will talk to us about situations which they don't want to discuss with anyone else. In any case, underlying their lives will be the whole teen scene in whatever form they experience it, with its assumptions about personal fulfilment, casual use of everything and anything with no consequences, and so on.

How do we listen?

Carefully! The old saying about having one mouth and two ears (and the need to use them in those proportions) is wise. When people talk to us we shouldn't jump in with our own comments, though we do need to show that we are listening. Watch people's body language as well as listening to their words.

We must also 'listen' by being alert to situations. If an individual keeps coming round 'just to chat' or stays with us like a shadow, they may well want to talk to someone. Are we appropriate? Then let's spend some time with them. If they write a note or a letter that needs talking about, we'll acknowledge receipt of it and fix a time to talk as soon as practicable.

There's often a temptation to try to cheer people up by saying things which are actually quite unhelpful. "I know how you feel", "It's part of growing up" and "You'll grow out of it" are all more or less guaranteed to make teenagers boil with rage or despair. That may seem a bit tough when all we're trying to do is make them feel better, but it's not all that surprising.

Where and when?

Late-night counselling sessions are a poor idea; it's better to make a time within the next day or two. And we should avoid one-to-one counselling of the opposite sex. Even if we're confident of (and right about) our own strength, it's a danger for the person we're talking to. Whichever sex we're with, we shouldn't get isolated. A quiet corner of a room in use or a room with an open door is best. Another adult needs to know what we are doing and where we will be.

Many of us may feel that, in practice, these precautions are unnecessary. That's fine until something goes wrong. Then it's indescribably horrible. The media and those who dislike the Church love scandals. Look at the fall-out from the Nine O'clock Service in Sheffield; evil things were done, and harvested down to the last gleanings. Let's not give anyone a chance to bring the gospel or the body of Christ into disrepute.

How much to take on

We cannot promise confidentiality beforehand. The situation may be something that we have to get help with. If an under-16 discloses an abusive situation, we are legally required to tell social services. If we do have to tell someone else, we should also tell the young person of our intended action.

We won't tell other people unnecessarily, but it's appropriate to 'off-load' to someone close, perhaps a church leader, if it's a big problem – we can be gripped by surprisingly strong emotions if a young person we know is undergoing bad things. It's right to admit when more expertise is needed and to support the young person through any further counselling they may have. It is important for us to say and demonstrate that we unconditionally love a young person, especially if they have told us something that they may feel has changed the way we will feel towards them.

And, of course...

We will pray: before we talk if it's an arranged time, while we talk and after we talk. If it's appropriate, we'll pray with the young person.

LET GO OF THAT TEENAGER!

Karen and Abigail, who had been the best of friends, quarrelled massively and both stopped coming to youth group in case they met.

Pete felt unaccepted by the church because of his habit of smoking cigarettes with unusual ingredients, and drifted away from the youth group because he identified it with church.

Catherine vanished, silent and sullen, from the group when she entered the sixth form, reappearing like a firework when she was converted at college.

Alex just opted out, partly because he found it hard to form friendships with the rest of the group and partly as a comment on his parents' high-profile and rather smothering faith.

People will leave our group, for all sorts of reasons. Some of the reasons will be connected with spiritual growth or decline; others won't. It can feel like a comment on how well we're doing as leaders. That's probably not true.

Our task is to be faithful in passing on a message. We trust God to use our life and our words to lead young people into a relationship with himself that will never end. But we know that neither our ministry nor the fellowship of the youth group will get them to heaven, but only the gracious Spirit of the living God. It is because we believe with all our hearts that we persevere, even when a youth group dwindles to nothing. As with Catherine in the examples given above, the seeds we've sown may come to life later in ways which we could not have dreamed of. We may never hear of it. Or we may, and then our joy will be hard to express.

The church as a whole may show little anxiety or disappointment if the youth group disappears, although it is considered to be a mark of an active and forward-looking church to have a positive ministry among young people. Perhaps there will be no more drama in services; perhaps the music group will be depleted; perhaps the Church Council will lose people elected to represent the 'youth viewpoint'. These things are soon accepted.

But we may face criticism. 'I can't think what they did with the youth group, to let all those young people just drift away!' Feelings of guilt, self-blame and despair may dog us.

However, it is part of the group growing up – even if the growth in some cases appears slight. Growth is painful and inevitable. We should accept that our young people become young adults, and not grieve for the lost relationships. New, adult bonds can arise if we can maintain contact with them in their emancipated state.

WAYS OF KEEPING IN TOUCH

1. Birthday cards. You will probably already know the birthdays of the group. Tactful questioning of parents or friends may well give you other dates. It is not difficult to put a card in the post. A contact of this sort is often appreciated especially when the person concerned doesn't have many cards anyway.

2. Occasional visits. Even a 'goodbye' visit, when the group leader in effect says, 'You have chosen to continue without us, but we have not forgotten you', may be helpful. Leaving a card with your address and phone number allows easy contact in time of need.

3. Hospitality. Think ahead about the possibility of giving hospitality. When an ex-group member is turned out of his flat, could he sleep for a couple of nights on your sitting-room floor?

4. Open door. Be available, if you can, for those occasions when there is a knock on the door and the wanderer returns. It's not always convenient, but a gentle and friendly welcome can reassure and sustain a developing adolescent.

5. Support. The church as a whole may still have contacts with group members. There will be engagements, weddings, baptisms in due course, and so on. Make sure your members know that you want (unobtrusively) to attend such events. Where an ex-member has relatives or parents in the congregation, ask them regularly, but in a relaxed way, how things are going.

6. Reunions. Occasional big events to which all past members of the group are invited may draw in people who would shy away from anything which hinted at regular contact.

7. Intercede. Finally, and most importantly, how do you pray for them? Do you have a prayer list through which you can pray for them regularly on a weekly or monthly basis? Do your ex-members know that when you say, 'I'll be praying for you,' you mean just what you say? Your ministry to them has not ceased; it has only changed.

One or more of these ideas can be invaluable in continuing to show love and concern for young people, who generally need reassurance that they are valued. However, be prepared for the fact that you will have to relinquish some of them altogether, to allow them to grow in forming new relationships. And realise that relinquishment is not a sign of failure on your part; it is a natural event that must and will come in the lives of some of your young people.

PASTORING OUR YOUNG PEOPLE

It won't have escaped your notice that this book emphasises the need to build relationships if our youth work is to be worthwhile. What is involved?

What should we be like?

We must be ourselves and we must be honest. Pretending won't get us anywhere, whether it's pretending we like them when we don't, pretending we like the same things they like, pretending we don't have any struggles with the Christian life, pretending we're stronger than we are, or whatever. Admitting that we have problems or that we're not into all the same things they like isn't, in most cases, going to destroy our relationship – just the opposite. They'll know what to expect and what our values really are. It may sometimes make us feel very exposed, but it's the only way to build trust and to encourage our young people to risk being vulnerable – and that's how they grow.

We must also be servants. Not so that the young people we're with never take responsibility, or so they get the feeling that following Jesus is just one long stint of being everybody's doormat, but because that's the approach Jesus took. See Mark 10:45. It's the way of the kingdom, as against the way of the world. The world will have plenty of chances to impress our members with how wonderful it is to be top of the heap. It may be only through us that they can see the joy and fulfilment of Christ's radically different approach.

We've said it before in this book, but it will bear repeating; if we talk a good gospel but don't live it out, they'll soon see through us anyway.

What are our young people like?

Let's see our young people lovingly but realistically! They are wonderfully valuable, because they're made in the image of God. They are full of potential, skills, creativity and all sorts of other gifts. It may take a while to dig down to these things with some of them, but it's true. They're also imperfect, prone to failure and wary of commitment. They may not be believers. We need to hold this balance between the wonderful and the fallen in our minds in all our dealings with them. Exaggerating the former can mean desperate disappointment at some stage in our relationship. Over-emphasizing the latter can mean that we never give them any scope to grow or take risks. It should not be beyond us to remember the two sides of the equation; it applies to us as well.

Us and them together

Many a youth leader has wandered onto dodgy paths by seeking the wrong things from the youth/leader relationship. Friendship is a worthy aim, but not friendship at all costs. It must be tempered with other things, because we have responsibilities to the group as a whole, to the church and to the gospel.

So there are times when friendship has to be qualified by the need to apply discipline. There are times when we must clearly model some aspect of Christ-like behaviour when a 'mate' would give up and just let things roll along. There are times when our greater experience of life will mean we have to take an approach which seems to emphasize that this relationship is not just one of friendship between equals. It's necessary. Do we want to produce Peter Pan, who never grew up, or Peter the apostle, who grew up with a thud and went on to bring much glory to God? No answer required.

And the church...

The church has a role to play in pastoring young people as well. It's often an unspoken assumption that only the youth team can have anything to do with the youth.

A member of the congregation approached the youth worker at the end of a service, asking that the young people gathered around the church door should not block the exit. The youth worker invited that person to go and ask the group personally. 'They're human and they're approachable.'

That's wise counsel. Any informal contact between young people and other church members is valuable and can begin to build lasting relationships. If the only communication between the church and the young people is through us, and is always bad news, the youth will feel rejected.

In formal ways, too, the church can play its part. Young people can be fitted into house groups, particularly over the summer if the youth group shuts down but other groups continue. At other times, a particular house group may pledge itself to pray for the work as a whole or for particular group members. Where lay people take part in services, group members and adults can be mixed in, to recognize that we're all in the same body of Christ.

See Pocket 8 for more thoughts on linking young people with the local church.

AUTHORITY AND DISCIPLINE

This is an area which can cause a lot of tension. We can end up torn between wanting to befriend the young people and feeling that they need a pretty strong rebuke. The way we want to treat an individual may conflict with the best interests of the group. So where do we start?

Biblical truths about people, authority and love must determine our approach to discipline.

People are made in God's image and are therefore precious, but we are fallen. Our fallen nature leads to polarity, tensions, conflict and rebellion (and the teenage years are often where these tendencies come to the surface most clearly). The twin truths of our value and our imperfection will keep us from harshness on the one hand and sentimentalism on the other.

We all live under **authority**. This is how God has designed the world. It is built into human existence. The Christian's supreme authority is the word of God, the Bible. As Christian leaders we are also responsible to other church leaders and parents. Our pattern for the exercise of authority is the Lord Jesus Christ. In him we see the perfect blend of authority and humility (Matthew 11:28-29).

Christian **love** is never soft and sentimental. It is always self-denying and sacrificial (John 13:1-17) and also prepared to correct and rebuke where necessary (Hebrews 12:5-11).

Putting it into practice

We need to apply these truths to the real human beings we work with. Most adolescents face an internal battle: wanting to see how far they can push the limits of what is allowed, yet wanting security which requires limits to be set; wanting desperately not to conform to adult patterns yet assimilating much from admired elders. *En bloc,* they are 'mixed-up kids' – but they're all still individuals.

These developmental needs may lure us towards one of two traps, both of which we need to avoid.

First is the trap of permissiveness. This is often fed by a fear that if any kind of discipline is imposed it will harm our relationship with a particular member. This is seldom so; in fact, the opposite is true. A teenager wants someone to look up to who will say when things are wrong. 'Anything goes' leads to disrespect and poor relationships.

The second trap is authoritarianism. This may be intended to ensure that the group runs smoothly, or we may just act this way for our own convenience. 'Lording it' over young people denies their personalities and may lead to a lack of initiative, independence and maturity. Authoritarianism is not the same as authority. The latter is necessary; the former very rarely is.

WOW! c

Spend more time praising good behaviour than punishing bad. Then members will learn to attract your attention by doing good things.

What, then, are some of the implications of these general principles?

● Remember the aim of the work: helping the young people to develop a fully mature faith. Let discipline serve this aim, not dictate to it, but be prepared to challenge group members over their behaviour where appropriate.

● Set standards, perhaps in consultation with the group members. The standards must be biblical, rational and justifiable; we must be able to give a reason for them other than 'Because I say so'! Communicate the standards and apply them consistently, because perceived favouritism can rip a group apart.

● Think ahead. Prepare for possible problems by thinking through situations that may arise. Be aware of what's happening in the young people's lives. Pray for wisdom.

● Love. We are dealing with individuals and there is no substitute for genuine concern. When we rebuke, we should follow it up with a friendly approach to reassure the young person that they are still loved and accepted.

● Don't compromise. Inaction on a particular occasion may be seen as condoning something undesirable. Above all, we must set an example in living by the standards we are encouraging the young people to follow.

WOW! c

Brothers, if someone is caught in a sin, you who are spiritual should restore him gently. But watch yourself, or you also may be tempted. (Galatians 6:1)

MANAGING THE GROUP

As well as maintaining discipline, we will have to consider other practical aspects of making sure the group provides the best possible environment for producing mature disciples. Such an environment is one where learning and relationships can happen naturally and over a period.

First, there are physical aspects which must be taken care of.

● We need to vary our approach, physical setting and so on, within reason. Group members can probably cope with and welcome more change than we can. Try to make the meeting room(s) friendly and comfortable, but with everyone visible when required. The setting should make group members feel they are recognised as more mature than lower age groups.

● Work and pray hard to get a helpful ratio of leaders to members. Match suitable leaders to particular members for specific activities, according to temperament, skills, etc.

● We must not (unless we have absolutely no option) speak over the group members or imply by other means that they are unimportant.

● Put particular effort into the first few minutes of a meeting, with firm control and a sense of purpose. Decide in advance how latecomers will be integrated. If they feel they have missed out on something good by being late, they are less likely to make a habit of it.

● Split into smaller groups sometimes – but know the cliques within the group!

Non-physical issues which need attention include:

● Understand how young people develop at different ages. Our 14-year-olds and 18-year-olds will think in different ways. Make decisions on the programme and learning methods accordingly, so that all ages feel they're being catered for.

● Be clear about the aims for the group, what is acceptable behaviour, etc. To this end, work towards a recognisable ethos and impetus for the group – use projects, outings and so on to develop this.

● Cultivate friendships outside group meetings, and be aware of members' home backgrounds. This makes relationships and learning easier and helps enormously in tackling any problems early.

● Value the group members and help them to value each other.

LINKING YOUNG PEOPLE INTO THE CHURCH

POCKET 8

Unless the youth group feels it has an important part to play in the whole life of the church and that its part is appreciated and its voice heard, divisions will grow and existing ones will not be healed.

TROUBLE AHEAD?

In the early 1980s, several branches of the Church produced reports which pointed out the absolute necessity for young people to feel valued, trusted and involved within the broader Church. The same point was still being made a dozen years later, for example in the *Youth A Part* report commissioned by the Church of England's General Synod and published in 1996.

The gap between what young people's vision for the Church and their experience of it has reached the point where Christians under 25 and those over 40 have little common ground. (That's a gross generalization, but true

in too many cases.) Hence the growth of a 'Christian youth sub-culture', sustained and serviced by a range of events and agencies outside the institutional structures of the churches.

Where 'youth churches' flourish in our neighbourhoods, or perhaps even more where there seems to be absolutely nothing intended specifically for young people, it may seem impossible that younger and older Christians can be brought together in a loving and developing fellowship. And yet this must be our constant aim; otherwise, as the older age groups in the church die off, there will be no one to replace them. That thought makes a mockery of the Bible's presentation of the Church as a body and a family.

HOW DO WE LEARN TOGETHER?

A common assumption is that the youth group needs teaching on a simplified and ultra-contemporary level ('How to be sure you're a Christian', 'The Christian attitude to out-of-town shopping centres') whereas older Christians can handle sterner stuff ('Studies in Philippians', 'The life of Gideon').

Certainly there's a difference between milk and meat, but we may see older

Christians wistfully eyeing the youth group programme, clearly wishing they could sneak in to get the benefit of what's on offer there; while Philippians and Gideon are rich enough subjects to yield both baby food and solids simultaneously if the preacher knows the job.

A bigger problem is that many adults have really ceased to learn, and teenagers perceive this. The older we grow, the more resistant we all become to taking on board new ideas and information. Many adult congregations gather week by week without any real expectation of finding out anything new from the Scriptures. At best, we hope to have our existing ideas confirmed. Young people see this and ask, 'What's the point in coming? You talk about the importance of teaching – but what difference does it really make?' Sadly, they seldom ask it out loud, and so our mutual incomprehension continues.

This is a great reason for involving the youth group in the church's home groups. When young people see older Christians openly discussing the Scriptures, they learn all sorts of useful lessons. 'So that's how you ask the right questions.' 'Wow, these people are disagreeing – perhaps one of them is wrong! So they still have things to learn!' And, of course, our young people will find the thrill and affirmation that comes from contributing to the process of a group which builds its members up from the word.

But how can we instil the right attitudes in our young people, to help them move towards learning together with the adults?

First, we can teach them a great deal about the corporateness of salvation. We are supposed to be members of one another. In the early church, this emphasis was built in from the word 'go'. Galatians 3:28 probably started life as a baptismal confession – so that, right at the moment of symbolic acceptance into the body of Christ, the new Christian proclaimed, 'We are all one in Christ Jesus'. It's easy for a youth evangelist or group leader to pour scorn on the irrelevance, greyness and out-of-date inflexibility of the church – and then present Jesus instead as exciting, up-to-date and personally satisfying. Such a strategy distances new Christians from the church and doesn't bode well for their future involvement with it.

Secondly, we can restrain the whiz-bang glamour of our normal youth group programme so that other church activities don't suffer too much by contrast. That's not to say that we shouldn't use the best resources available in our work with young people. But unless they get used to experiencing no-frills, plain, honest sessions of learning and working in the youth group context, how are they ever to relate to that kind of thing in the local church? If every week in the youth fellowship they have come to expect a succession of bigger and better firework displays, how will they ever learn to switch to the less exciting discipline of all-age church activities?

Thirdly, we can teach them how to use older Christians as resources. We can refrain from posing as the fount of all wisdom when they come to us with questions, and say instead, 'Good question. Why don't you ask Mr So-and-So? He knows a lot about that. I'll introduce you if you like...'

Fourthly, we can encourage our church to be just a teensy bit livelier. Just occasionally, though; hey, we're realists.

Finally, we can take active steps to involve older people with the youth group programme as special guests, interviewees, camp houseparents, hosts for youth activities. (But make sure that if you take the youth group to their home they don't hide in the kitchen all night making endless cups of coffee. Interaction and exposure are what we want.)

STEPPING INTO CHURCH

Clearly, youth group members who are Christians should be baptized. Much can be made of this as an adult service if it did not take place in infancy. If they were baptized as children, for several reasons there is a need for a service in which to profess faith publicly and be welcomed into full membership of the church. There is the theological need for faith to be started by the individual for himself. There is the need for the church openly to welcome a new, adult member. There may well also be the individual's own felt need to nail his or her colours publicly to the mast. The form this service takes is a complex question, which we cannot deal with here. Some churches will have a confirmation service, others will provide something else. It is important that we don't let our young people feel that they have missed out if they were baptized as infants – baptism is about God's activity, not our response – but it is important that they have an outlet for declaring their faith.

The timing of admission to communion is another complex issue, though it would seem right biblically to encourage this as soon as people declare their faith publicly and have been welcomed by the church. The time lapse between baptism in infancy and a later personal response ought not to worry us. Nor should remarks like, 'I became a Christian at my baptism' (meaning, in infancy) as opposed to, 'I became a Christian last week when I gave my life to Christ.' It is similar to saying, 'He became a soldier today when he enlisted' and his commanding officer saying of him six months later after hard training, 'I have made a soldier of so-and-so'. Both are true, in differing senses.

GROWING INTO CHURCH

If we want to see our young people grow into a full, adult appreciation of all that church membership means – to walk successfully across the bridge out of the group and into the adult church – then to our carefully crafted teaching sessions we will have to add some degree of discipline. Unless they grow to see their faith as necessarily involving a programme of training in godliness, administered to them by their contacts with the rest of the body of Christ, we will be breeding passengers, supporters, sympathisers, but not disciples.

So how do we do it? How can young people be drawn gradually into the discipline of local church membership? It will, of course, happen more easily in a church which has already thought seriously about 'training in godliness', and has instituted systems to make it work for all age groups, not just the young. But are there any general principles which can help?

Five factors are involved. The first is **our own example**. It's easy to give the impression that our dear minister is out of touch and hundreds of years out of date but never mind, kids, I'm the knight in shining armour who is fighting for your freedom. But we must demonstrate our own loyalty to our leaders, even when we disagree with them and the young people know it! 'Loyalty' is meaningless when our leaders are asking us to do what we'd have chosen to do anyway. Real loyalty is tested when they ask us to go against our inclinations.

The second factor in creating a readiness for discipline is the **response of the church** to the presence of the young people in their midst. The kind of welcome they get determines the kind of loyalty they show. The church which accepts young people readily as 'one in Christ Jesus' with themselves will not find it hard to retain their loyalty. The two perils are first that adult church members will persist in treating teenagers as children, and secondly that they will stand in awe of These Dear Young People and start pandering to their wishes rather than challenging them to growth.

The third factor involved is the **expectations of the young people** themselves. How often do we teach our young people about the subject of loyalty to leadership, discipline, training in godliness? If the answer is 'never', we're producing a group which will have only the vaguest glimmer of awareness about what leaders are there for, how they contribute to the health of the church and what importance they have for the young Christian's spiritual development.

The fourth factor is **our willingness as youth leaders to invest our time wisely**. Other adults will not have as much time to be thrown into contact with the teenagers as we will. Thus it is important for as much to be made of that contact as possible. Every time a young person meets a leader is important. It is our job to use some of our time to plan these encounters, to work to make them as valuable and frequent as possible, to make sure that no one is able to graduate from our youth work and say truthfully, 'But I never really had the chance to get to know the church leaders'.

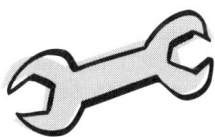

Think back over the past three months. How much of it was invested in activities that led to significant, life-building encounters between young people and the church leaders?

The final factor is **our ability to stand within an adult world and relate credibly to teenagers**; to be able to make bridges between adults in the church and the young people in our charge. This is a trump card we can play in either of two ways.

The first way is to use our ability to make everyone – old and young – stand in awe of us. The older group will say, 'It's amazing how good he is with those young people.' And the young people think, 'Nobody else has any time for us, but Fred's all right.' (If you are neither male nor called Fred, please don't take offence; just use your imagination. Thank you.)

The problem with this approach is that it leaves us with a king-size ego, a youth group so dependent on us that they never join the church, and no chance at all of convincing the other adults that teenagers are human beings. We will in fact have daunted them; if it takes all Fred's gifts to build a relationship with young people, what chance does a less talented adult stand? Better not to try – leave it to Fred. (But when he leaves, the church will be Fredbare!)

Alternatively, we can use our trump card to build a two-way channel of communication, gradually bringing the young people and the church leaders closer and closer together, so that in the life of any individual young person the original gap of sympathy and comprehension is closed completely and it becomes possible for the teenager to feel at home with the leaders. As the gap closes, we can step out of the middle and leave them face to face.

Of course, this sounds easier than it really is. Neither party may appreciate our scheming to throw them together. And when we do get them together, we have to brace ourselves for disappointments. The teenager may say the wrong thing and scandalize the leader, or perhaps clam up completely. The leader may feel insecure and start treating the teenager like a five-year-old, or perhaps also clam up completely!

But let's work at it. There are too many Christian teenagers whose sole contact with the leaders of their church has been five unrealistic and embarrassed confirmation classes. Or listening to an occasional talk at the youth fellowship from one of the wardens (who isn't particularly good at this sort of thing, but feels it's a duty he must occasionally fulfil...).

Small wonder that in such environments young people of promise sometimes fail to develop into adult church members. Now, some of our best young people may fail too. But it needn't be for this reason, need it?

POCKET 9

SERIOUS BUILDING

HOW TO MAKE DISCIPLES OUT OF THE YOUTH GROUP

Conversion is only the first step in a walk with God. The Apostle Paul treated his converts as part of his family: he didn't just hit them with the gospel and then abandon them. We need follow-up as well as evangelism. This should be one unified job, seeing Christ formed in people. The moment of accepting Christ is just the gateway to a continuing process. We should be just as much involved in follow-up as in getting people to make the decision in the first place.

Because evangelicals tend to stress the personal side of salvation, we can sometimes forget that we are responsible for one another. If we lead someone, particularly a member of our youth group, to Christ then we are in a position of special responsibility for that person.

For many of us there is nothing more exciting than making people see Christ. But if anything is more exciting it is what happens after that. That's the job which, as youth leaders, we are privileged to do for members of our groups who have found Christ through our ministry. After making people see him the job is to make people resemble him. Real satisfaction in our ministry is when we see young people's minds, emotions and wills being re-orientated so that Jesus appears in the midst of their lives.

How did Jesus do it?

The way Jesus worked gives us some idea of the kind of job we are supposed to be doing. **He spent time with his disciples.** How much time do we spend with those who become Christians through our group, apart from in group meetings? How often are we with them on purely social occasions? **Jesus prayed for his disciples.** How much time do we invest in prayer for those who become Christians through our group? **Jesus challenged his disciples.** He gave them jobs to do, continually pushing them out into activity and responsibility, giving them the freedom to fail. How much do we challenge our members, egging them on to continued growth with new challenges and options? **Jesus took his disciples with him** on most of his travelling, so that they could learn by watching him in action. It can be painful to let young people watch us doing jobs, especially when we mess things up. But they will learn by watching us in action. **Jesus pushed his disciples out into service.** How far are our group members emotionally dependent on us as leaders, and how far do we manage to cut the apron strings so that they become able to stand as free, mature, Christian adults in their own right?

Learning to learn

The new Christian's mind has to be changed. People's minds matter (Romans 12:1-2). It's when God gets into our thought patterns and we start thinking in a different way from most people in the world that we find things happening in our Christian lives. However, this first step in the discipling process is more than an academic issue. Transforming the mind is more than teaching doctrine.

When we look at the way Jesus taught, we can see that there was no divorce between the mind and life; what was going on in the mind was being worked out through the hands and feet. We learn more by trying things out than by simply putting more information into our brains.

We train people's minds for freedom, not so that we can squash their ability to think for themselves. We want to breed independence of thought. Often our

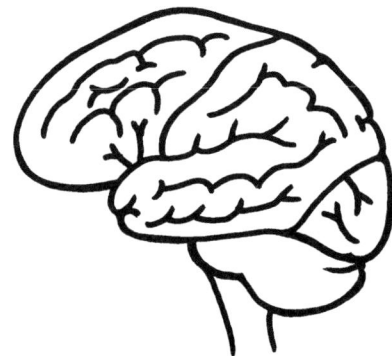

young people, growing up in an age of instant communication and immediate action, shy away from the need to reflect on issues and want to be told what to think. If we give them a set of attitudes to adopt and an identity to take on, that may be fine by them, because the temptation for an adolescent is always to conform. Although we will want to be good models for them we don't want to produce clones. The only mature Christianity relies on God, not on humans. So we train people's minds, challenging them to think.

Learning to love

The emotions need to be transformed as well. Young people tend to be emotional so this can be an easy challenge to make. There are dangers in that, but

Learning to live

The will is the area we neglect more than any other. The whole business of living for Christ at the level of day-to-day obedience, is what we're most likely to miss out.

It is easy to work at the level of the emotions and then, once an emotional response has been made, to move on to the level of the mind and say, 'You need to learn this, this and this'. It is much more difficult to work at the level of the will and say, 'Now, this is how you are supposed to live'. People learn at that level by watching us. Paul told people to imitate him, not because he was big-headed but because he was practical and knew that people were going to imitate him anyway. The most costly part of being a leader is opening up and showing a pattern, a way of

when people become Christians their emotions need to be opened up. They need to learn to love God. That's a difficult thing to teach. 'Worship times' are often stilted in the youth group because even when young people love God they may not know how to show it. It is probably easier to help people in smaller groups than large ones, and it probably helps to expose members to very large events where they won't feel the attention is on them at all.

Our young disciples also need to learn to love other people. People today hide from one another. We are trained from early childhood to put on masks. When people turn to Christ, one of the most difficult things to teach is to open up to others. We cannot do it in the youth group alone – it is a job for the whole church. Showing young people that they are one with the 89-year-olds, the silly kids coming out of Sunday School and the middle-aged businessmen with whom they have nothing in common is difficult. But in the end it is the secret of permanence and success. Training them to love people to whom they don't naturally relate is the way of making effective disciples.

living, which the next generation can latch onto and turn into a committed form of Christian discipleship for themselves.

Spotting difficulties

There are certain specific hindrances in leading young people to become disciples. One is the importance of young people in society today. The youth market is worth thousands of millions of pounds each year. Young people have a huge importance in society's eyes. We must be careful not to be led to idolize the young, putting them on a pedestal above older sectors of the population and giving them a status they don't deserve. It is very easy just to assent in the attitudes of society towards young people, but this doesn't help them.

A second hindrance is that when young people commit themselves they do it on the basis of limited freedom and limited experience of the world. They don't understand all the stresses and strains that life will bring (though we won't make ourselves popular by pointing this out!). They also commit themselves on the basis of limited self-knowledge, and we need to bear this in mind.

A third hindrance is identity. The adolescent years are when people are finding out for themselves who they are. They try out different roles to find out what fits their personality. That's why someone in school can be a skinhead one week and a heavy metal freak the next (if his hair grows very quickly!). So a group is very important because it gives security and identity. We can use that wrongly or we can use it to build real bonds between the young people and the church.

FOSTERING GROUP MEMBERS' GIFTS

Somewhere in our group, at some stage, we'll have someone who will later move into a position of leadership in the church. It will probably happen quite a lot, and to apparently unlikely people. Pray that it does. And ponder for a while on how we can help that person or those people to grow their leadership skills. Other people in the group will have other abilities; artistic, musical, teaching, pastoral and so on. Those gifts may be in their very early days. How can we help them to grow?

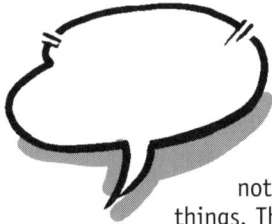

When Steve was a curate he resolved to spend six months watching and not changing things. Then he heard the CYFA music group. They were bad. The bats in the belfry all left. But he stuck to his resolve. After six months they became quite good. The main reason was a congregation supportive of young people trying things out.

Think of the process by which you have come to lead your current youth work, from the earliest days of your involvement in Christian things. What people, events and opportunities gave you the chance to use your abilities more fully so that eventually you came to be a leader?

What can we do to help?

Give opportunities. It is rather easy for us to be possessive about leadership and about doing the 'up-front' things in the group. It takes courage to let others, especially group members, develop in these roles. Yet it is how the next generation of leaders will grow, to the good of the church and the glory of God.

Devote time to encouraging people. Those with gifts may not have the confidence to use them at first. Our loving and gentle insistence, doing things alongside them at first and being ready to take a more or less active role according to how things work out, will be crucial in helping them make full use of the abilities God has given them.

Champion group members against those who are unwilling to let them use their gifts. There will always be people who don't trust them or are not secure enough to step aside, even for a short time, so that the young people have some space to work. If we succeed in gaining an opportunity for our young people to use their gifts and something goes wrong, we must be willing to take the blame and criticism. And then fight for another chance for them.

Ways to unearth gifts

If we build relationships with the group, we should automatically find out many of the abilities our members have. However, this will happen only if fostering gifts and leadership in them is on our agenda; that is, we see them as more than just 'the people we teach'. Let's look far ahead for them, and be ambitious that they will do great things, starting now.

Skills Olympics

Stage a number of different events: sketch the leader, get a tune out of a new instrument, pick the main point out of a Bible passage, make a model of the Archbishop of Canterbury out of Play-Doh and so on.

Emergency Church

Ask the group to imagine that everyone with a defined role in the church (including musicians, flower arrangers etc) has been kidnapped by terrorists. Leaving aside the question of whether the group would pay a ransom to get them back, ask them to nominate group members to fulfil all the different roles. Perhaps you could negotiate with the church leader for those group members to job-share for a week with those who actually fulfil the functions.

OUR LEADER

POCKET 10

PASSING MUSTER AND PASSING ON

EVALUATION

"I don't know where we're going, but we're sure getting there fast!" The pace of youth work is certainly furious and it is vital occasionally to review its direction. What are we actually trying to achieve? Are we achieving it? Are we using the best methods?

Why should we try to evaluate our work? A large part of the reason is connected to our need to keep a long-term perspective on what we're doing: that Last Day syndrome again! Part of what our Lord and King will look at is the work we've done: its content and quality (1 Corinthians 3:12-15). So, not in guilty fear but in the desire to be congratulated by Jesus on his return for what we've done in his name, we need to keep an eye on how we're doing.

Success

Many of us are confused about what constitutes success or failure in our youth work. Here are one youth group's suggestions. They may not exactly mirror what your own group would say, but they're probably fairly typical.

WHAT MAKES A SUCCESSFUL YOUTH GROUP?

If the group is receptive it helps. It also helps if there is a social mix, so you don't just get 30 middle-class kids sitting in chairs and nodding at everything the leader says – variety is the spice of life.

Vision.

Good, enthusiastic leaders.

Fun and games.

Nice women.

A young youth leader, fun people and something to do.

Food.

Friendly atmosphere. Relaxed – no pressure to have to do anything.

Being kind and having someone to talk to. Also leaders who try not to keep things from you.

Music.

Unjudgmental leaders.

Leaders who treat you as friends, some organization but some freedom. Decent facilities and equipment, everyone friendly – no bitching.

Sexy, long-haired boys who play the guitar.

People who care for each other and don't judge each other.

Trust.

Going places and doing things.

Wanting to know more about God.

WHAT MAKES AN UNSUCCESSFUL YOUTH GROUP?

The opposite of all the above, and also:

When the kids won't mix and when the leaders can't reach them on their own level.

No one mixing and talking with each other.

Leaders who are awful to you and don't tell you things properly.

Nasty leaders who make you do things you don't want to.

Patronizing leaders.

Sexy, long-haired boys who play the guitar being too godly.

So, where does that leave us? Probably feeling under a good deal of pressure, given the emphasis on leaders' qualities that emerges.

Where, then, shall we fix our gaze? Well, let's first make sure that we don't fix it on success itself. American youth worker Paul Borthwick says: "We lose our spiritual direction when we make it our priority to pursue the elusive target called success."* The direction of our gaze needs to be Godwards. Looking to God means looking to the end of all our work: the glory which awaits us through God's grace. Paul's letters to the Corinthians were written against a background of rejection and resistance within that church, which was so dear to him and in which he'd invested so much emotional capital. And yet he wrote, "Therefore we do not lose heart. Though outwardly we are wasting away, yet inwardly we are being renewed day by day. For our light and momentary troubles are achieving for us an eternal glory that far outweighs them all." (2 Corinthians 4:16-17)

That long-term view is essential if we are to keep the gains and losses of our youth work in proper perspective. Given that right directing of our vision, we can see that failure in our youth work is not having low numbers in our group or the absence of wall-to-wall wacky activities or of a continual, high level of excitement. Nor is success the presence of high numbers or the provision of such activities. We seek to honour God, and to produce people who will honour him in the long term.

At the time of writing this, I've just planted some bulbs in my garden. I'd love to see them in flower tomorrow – but I won't. The flowers will take time to appear. And that's assuming that I did the planting properly – right depth, right position, right way up and so on. I'm quite capable of getting all those things wrong, and then the bulbs will come to nothing. The same basic principle applies in our youth work. The results are very seldom seen straight away, and the key thing for us is to do the work properly. Judged by immediate results, all I've got for my trouble is a couple of muddy patches in my lawn. Judged by immediate results, much of our youth work will seem a bit of an unfruitful mess.

So let's plant the bulbs, sow the seed, or use any other metaphor which reminds us that the work is a long-term one and that we are not responsible for its eventual outcome. Success for us is doing that groundwork well. It means teaching Scripture clearly and accurately, so that our young people can see that it applies to them and their world and can come to Jesus as Saviour and Lord. It means forming relationships; nourishing and plugging away at them even when we're exhausted and discouraged and never want to see anyone under the age of 75 again in the whole of our lives. And we will sometimes fail in these things – but that doesn't disqualify us from going on and getting it right in future. Jesus reinstated Peter after his denial. God can still use us even if we let him down.

Obviously we need to listen to what our group members tell us about what they like and what attracts them to come along. But let's make those things our servants, not our masters. Our Father loves to see his people becoming more like his Son, with the Son's characteristics, values and attitudes. Those are the things he blesses. Those are the things that lead to success in our work.

And now?

You could...

Find time to read a book on the principles of Christian youth work or on the qualities we need as Christian leaders. You'll find suggestions in the booklist at the end of this book.

Read and pray about Philippians 3:7-11; a key and beautiful passage which puts the world's assessment of success and achievement into perfect, godly perspective.

Remember, 'My grace is sufficient for you, for my power is made perfect in weakness' (2 Corinthians 12:9). And rejoice!

How do we judge?

It is a mistake to think that growth is the only (or main) measure of success in youth work. Small numbers may mean that God is teaching us perseverance and patience, or giving us a chance to build especially deep relationships with the few he's given us for the time being. And a new harvest may be just around the corner.

As a minor point to consider when thinking about growth, it is a general (though not universal) fact that it is

*Feeding your Forgotten Soul, pub. Youth Specialties Books (US) 1990

easier to attract girls to our groups than boys. A group of ten girls will not attract an equivalent number of boys, but the reverse is often true. 'A group that is bigger than ten, and contains more boys than girls, will probably grow despite you' (Steve Tilley, Head of CYFA). It is wise to be aware of this tendency and greater effort may have to be expended on building up the boys' side of the work. Boys up to the age of 16 tend to be games/activities-orientated. And food always attracts.

It's good to ask members of the group how they think things are going. The danger, of course, is that we'll fall into the trap of courting popularity. We need to be prepared to hear some criticism and to respond appropriately, not being deflecting from our strategy for the group if it's misplaced but taking it into account if it's merited.

Our church leaders should also be involved in evaluating the work. If we keep them informed as we go along and if they have at least occasional contacts with the group they'll have a better idea of how we're doing.

Here are some big questions you might use in a leaders' meeting to assess the progress of your youth work. They pick up many of the main themes we have considered in this book.

● Is your youth work integrated into the whole church, and so building up the body of Christ?

● Are you caring properly for the spiritually hungry core group?

● Are you opening yourself to your young people in life-to-life discipleship?

● Are you focusing your own ministry on those you can really help?

● Are you taking time to review and assess your aims and objectives?

● Is there any area of youth work mentioned in this book that you are neglecting?

● Are you praying?

HANDING OVER

Every time we give something up we undergo a kind of bereavement, and the youth work will be no different, whether we step gracefully aside at the age of 83 or are dragged kicking and screaming from the scene in our twenties in order to look after the church's new billiard-hall-cum-dolphinarium scheme for reaching unchurched pool sharks.

Although we've stressed the need for commitment and continuity, that's not the same as hanging on too long when it's time to quit. To put a serious gloss on the last paragraph, giving up may be a natural thing, a result of staleness, or an inevitable consequence of a new calling to serve God in a different way. Whatever the cause, it will almost always hurt. So let's be prepared for that. It doesn't mean we have to dwell gloomily on the sad day that lies somewhere ahead, but acknowledging that it will come is a help in approaching it calmly and positively.

The best way to hand over the youth work is to plan it. Give new leaders time to prepare and perhaps have a hand-over period when the group can get to trust a new leadership while still having the comfort and security of your presence. During this time, it may be that some group members will plead with you to stay on, or take the line, "They're not as good as you..." Don't be sidetracked by that kind of thing: if your decision has been made with prayer for wisdom and you're confident about the new leaders, there's no need to change your mind. (Equally, if the group say, "They're far better than you; push off quickly," try not to be discouraged...)

Should you stay on the scene, in the background perhaps, after handing over? Probably not. By all means let the new leaders know that they can consult you if they wish to, and actively encourage them to supply you with material for prayer, but actually to attend the group will probably be a distraction and make people feel uncomfortable.

Pray for those who led the youth work before you, if there were any, in the ministry or well-earned rest they've moved on to.

Pray regularly for wisdom about your own future course, and that you'll know the right time and way to hand over the youth work.

Pray for your work in the meantime, reflecting on things you have learned from this book. May God bless your work. Amen.

RESOURCES

There are zillions of books and other resources for youth leaders, on all sorts of topics. This is just a starter pack, skimming the surface of the best and most recent.

Youth ministry
Christian Youth Work – A Strategy for Youth Leaders
Mark Ashton and Phil Moon
Monarch 1995

Youthwork and How To Do It – The Oxford Youth Works Guide to Working with Young People
Pete Ward, Sam Adams and Jude Levermore
Lynx 1994

Evangelism
Outside In – Reaching Un-churched Young People Today
Mike Breen
Scripture Union 1993

Ventures, Camps, Houseparties and Residential Work
Get Away – How to Take Your Youth Group Away and Survive
Arlo Reichter and others
Bible Society 1991

Sex and Relationships
...and God Created Sex!
Chick Yuill
Monarch 1995

The Seduction
Paul Francis
Marshall Pickering 1995

The Bible
Starting with the Old Testament – a Lion First Guide
Starting with the New Testament – a Lion First Guide
Stephen Travis
Lion 1994

Bible Reading Notes for Teenagers
The Ichthus File – the Bible Fair and Square
St Matthias Press
(New issue every couple of months)

Dayzd – 90 Days Bible Reading Guides
(4 books)
Scripture Union 1997

Worship
Worship and Youth Culture – A Guide to Making Services Radical and Relevant
Pete Ward
Marshall Pickering 1993

Rave On!
Simon Heathfield
CPAS 1994

DIY Worship
Simon Heathfield
CPAS 1996

Games and Ideas
The New Youth Games Book
Alan Dearling and Howie Armstrong
Russell House Publishing 1994

Youthwork Ideas – Ideas, Resources and Guidance for Youth Ministry
John Buckeridge
Kingsway 1993

Prayer
A Bunch of Green Bananas – Ideas for Teenagers which may Ripen into Prayer
David Gatward
Kevin Mayhew Ltd 1993